Using your
Computer
The **beginner's** guide

Second Edition

© Haynes Publishing 2003
Reprinted 2004
Second edition published 2006
Reprinted 2007

Published by: Haynes Publishing
Sparkford, Yeovil, Somerset BA22 7JJ
Tel: 01963 442030 Fax: 01963 440001
Int. tel: +44 1963 442030 Fax: +44 1963 440001
E-mail: sales@haynes.co.uk
Website: www.haynes.co.uk

British Library Cataloguing in Publication Data:
A catalogue record for this book is available from the British Library

ISBN 978 1 84425 350 0

Printed in Britain by J. H. Haynes & Co. Ltd, Sparkford

Throughout this book, trademarked names are used. Rather than put a trademark symbol after every occurrence of a trademarked name, we use the names in an editorial fashion only, and to the benefit of the trademark owner, with no intention of infringement of the trademark. Where such designations appear in this book, they have been printed with initial caps.

Whilst we at J. H. Haynes & Co. Ltd strive to ensure the accuracy and completeness of the information in this manual, it is provided entirely at the risk of the user. Neither the company nor the author can accept liability for any errors, omissions or damage resulting therefrom. In particular, users should be aware that component and accessory manufacturers, and software providers, can change specifications without notice, thus appropriate professional advice should always be sought.

Using your
Computer
The beginner's guide
Second Edition

Kyle MacRae

For PCs running **Windows XP** Home Edition

Contents

Introduction

So you've finally taken the plunge and bought yourself a PC – or perhaps had one foisted upon you by an impatient offspring? Well, congratulations! May we say that you couldn't have picked a better time for it. Relatively speaking, today's personal computer is cheaper, smarter and vastly more powerful than those of yesteryear … but that's all by the by. What matters more in the present context is that it's much easier to get to grips with a computer than ever before.

It's getting better all the time.

For all its many marvels, the average personal computer has long been over-complicated, counter-intuitive and prone to doing the dumbest things at times. However, the introduction of Windows XP Home Edition, an operating system developed by Microsoft for domestic PCs, has gone a long way towards bridging the gap

between a computer's capability and its usability. More often than not, you will discover that your PC will 'just work' – and that's a remarkable step forward in computer evolution.

The real keys to understanding your new machine are taking things slowly and keeping it simple. This is why you won't find us pointing out ten different ways to do everything. Rather, we'll concentrate exclusively on the absolute essentials and tackle each new subject in jargon-free plain English.

In time, you will doubtless want to learn more about your computer and what it can do for you. We would certainly encourage this: invoke the help of friends or colleagues, undertake a course in computing, or just spend a little time experimenting. But our present aim, while modest, is giving you the know-how you need to begin using your computer.

We will assume from the outset that you know next to, or absolutely, nothing about computers. Much of what follows will therefore appear trivial to those with some practical experience under their belts. But they can look elsewhere. This is unashamedly a manual for the complete beginner.

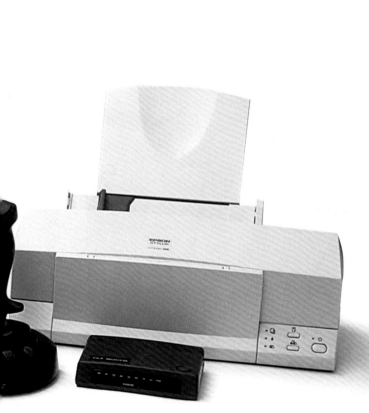

A personal note

I once worked as a computer consultant, helping newcomers to buy, set up and use their first PC. One afternoon, I found myself plugging together a client's brand new state-of-the-art computer system – an exuberant and ill-advised (though not by me) purchase which had set him back some ludicrous sum. When all was ready, I handed over the reins – well, the mouse – and proclaimed: 'OK, click the Start button and let's get going!'

Some 40 minutes later (I kid you not), we were still sat at that desk, trying repeatedly, desperately but ultimately unsuccessfully to make that click. For the avoidance of doubt, this client was a retired professional with dextrous hands, perfectly good eyesight and the full complement of faculties. But he just could not relate the movements of a slithery lump of plastic on a rubber mat to those of a pointer on his PC's monitor screen. I shared his frustration as the pointer darted around the screen from corner to corner, beyond his control and beyond his ken; and I may even have echoed his soft curse when finally the pointer came close enough to the Start button to hazard a speculative click … only for the mouse to wobble in his hand and send the pointer skating across the screen once more.

It struck me then, as it strikes me now, that there is a pressing need for a practical guide that makes no assumptions whatsoever about the relationship between a computer and its owner. A mouse is not an intuitive way to control a computer, any more than pressing a pedal is an intuitive way to make a car go faster, or stop; these things have to be taught, learned and practised, not taken for granted and glossed over.

This, then, is the book written for the frustrated 'newbie' who really wants to use a computer but isn't quite sure where to start … and doesn't fancy taking a degree in geekology just to be able to send an e-mail.

How to use this book

For the sake of consistency and clarity, we will use certain conventions throughout this manual.

Mouse instructions

When you see the ✍ symbol, we are referring to an action performed with the mouse. So, for instance,

✍ *Start*

means 'use the mouse to move the on-screen pointer to the Start button, and click it'.

Furthermore, most mouse-driven actions involve several steps. Each step starts on a new line. As a rule, when we say 'click', we mean click the left mouse button once.
Don't worry – this will become clear soon enough.

There are two other mouse actions, double click and right button click. All three actions appear as follows;

✍ *Single click on the left mouse button*

✍ *Double click on the left mouse button*

✍ *Single click on the right mouse button*

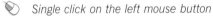

Screen examples

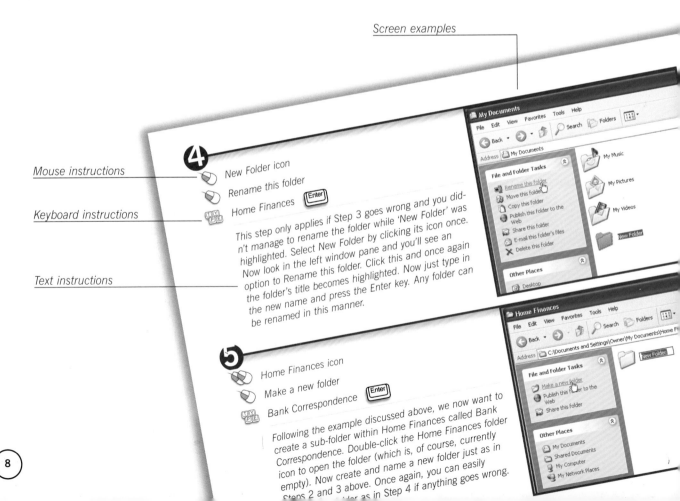

Mouse instructions

Keyboard instructions

Text instructions

✍ New Folder icon
✍ Rename this folder
⌨ Home Finances [Enter]

This step only applies if Step 3 goes wrong and you didn't manage to rename the folder while 'New Folder' was highlighted. Select New Folder by clicking its icon once. Now look in the left window pane and you'll see an option to Rename this folder. Click this and once again the folder's title becomes highlighted. Now just type in the new name and press the Enter key. Any folder can be renamed in this manner.

✍ Home Finances icon
✍ Make a new folder
⌨ Bank Correspondence [Enter]

Following the example discussed above, we now want to create a sub-folder within Home Finances called Bank Correspondence. Double-click the Home Finances folder icon to open the folder (which is, of course, currently empty). Now create and name a new folder just as in Steps 2 and 3 above. Once again, you can easily ... der as in Step 4 if anything goes wrong.

Keyboard instructions

When you see the symbol, the directions refer to the keyboard. For example:

 teapot

means 'type the word "teapot" on the keyboard now'. Type exactly what you see, being sure to note any spaces or unusual symbols.

However, when the direction is contained within square brackets, this indicates that you should type something that pertains to you specifically e.g.

 [your e-mail address]

means 'type in your own e-mail address'. We'll soon have you using the keyboard with abandon.

When we want you to press a certain key on the keyboard, this is denoted by means of a box. Thus

 ⌈Enter⌉

means 'press the Enter key'.

Where an action requires you to press more than one key simultaneously, we use the + symbol to link them. Thus

is an instruction to press the three named keys at the same time. And it really doesn't get any more complicated than that!

Text instructions

Beneath the mouse and keyboard directions, we explain the purpose and method of each step in more detail. Please read these instructions in full before clicking the mouse or typing on the keyboard.

Jargon

Any word or phrase highlighted like *this* is fully explained in the glossary. This helps to keep the main text clear of non-essential clutter. To avoid an over-complicated appearance, we only highlight the first occurrence of the word or phrase.

Screen examples

We also make frequent use of 'screenshots' to illustrate the effect of a given procedure. However, it is not always possible to show every single step along the way so be sure to follow the mouse, keyboard and text instructions carefully.

Windows Vista

This manual has been written for Windows XP. However, you may be aware that Microsoft is launching a new 'operating system (see p.15) in 2007, called Windows Vista. We'll bring out a Windows Vista version of this manual in due course. For now, though, Windows XP is almost certainly what you'll encounter when you turn on your first PC. This second edition of Using Your Computer has been completely updated to include all the latest XP features, and it will set you up perfectly for a later transition to Vista.

1

PART  # From delivery to desktop

Let's assume that you've just taken delivery of several rather large and heavy panic-inducing boxes. If you had just bought a television set or some hi-fi equipment, you could be reasonably confident of connecting a couple of cables, plugging it into the mains electricity and being able to sit back and enjoy the fruit of your labours. But this is a computer system, and you just *know* that it's going to stress you out.

Perhaps you've already called your colleagues, neighbours or the emergency services for assistance. But relax. In just a few pages time, you'll be using your PC for the very first time. We're going to talk you through unpacking and setting up your shiny new computer system so that it works first time around … and keeps on working.

PART ① A (very) potted guide to PCs

Be honest, now – how much do you really want to know about your computer? You don't have to grasp the workings of an internal combustion engine to drive a car or comprehend the mysteries of twisted-pair copper wiring to pick up the telephone. Most computer manuals (in our admittedly biased opinion) go into far too much detail, leaving you a good deal more knowledgeable but not necessarily better equipped to do something useful like writing a letter. So here instead is a brief look at the basics. We'll get through it as quickly as we possibly can.

Your computer system is essentially composed of two parts, hardware and software.

Hardware

First, let's consider the nuts and bolts.

The system unit Or, if you prefer, the case. System units are usually tall, thin 'tower' affairs these days but you can still buy squat, wide cases called, confusingly, 'desktop' PCs. There is no practical difference between the two aside from the design; a desktop PC is basically a tower case on its side. See illustration below.

The system unit has two important buttons on the front: an on/off switch, and a reset switch. The first controls the power supply to the computer, and the second is used to *restart* the computer if it ever 'hangs' i.e. freezes in the middle of an operation. Windows XP has largely made this hassle a thing of the past.

Inside the system unit is a large printed circuit board known as the motherboard, or mainboard. This hosts the *processor* and *memory* and all the other electronic gubbins that make a computer smart. Everything that plays a part in your computer system connects to the *motherboard* in one way or another.

Monitor

Speakers

Keyboard

Mouse

CD/DVD drive

Floppy disc drive

System unit

On/off switch

Reset switch

Peripherals

If the system unit is the PC proper, everything else can be called a peripheral device. But what does it all do?

Monitor A display screen on which you view images generated by your computer. Virtually all monitors now are lightweight flat-screen LCD models, whereas old monitors used a bulky, heavy CRT technology.

Keyboard A typewriter-like input device. Every press of a key generates a signal that the computer interprets and acts upon. Basically, it's one way of feeding instructions to your computer.

Mouse This handheld input device controls a pointer on the monitor screen. By pointing at on-screen objects and clicking the mouse's buttons, you make your computer do stuff. This is the other way of feeding instructions to your computer.

Speakers Without speakers, your computer can emit only the odd forlorn bleep. With speakers, it rocks.

Printer A device that turns computer-generated content into paper documents. Thus you might write a letter or draw a picture on your computer and print out a hard copy on your printer. Inkjet printers print in colour and are ideal for family use; laser printers generally print in black and white only but achieve a higher quality suitable for professional stationery.

Scanner A device that takes a photograph of anything you place under the lid, turns it into an electronic image and sends it to your computer. Ideal for scanning snapshots or documents.

Drives

A drive is a device that reads *data* from and, sometimes, writes data to magnetic or optical media. In plain English, drives let you access and save information.

Hard disk drive At the heart of any PC is the hard *disk* drive. This is where files you create are saved. It is also home to the computer's operating system and application software, more of which shortly. Without a hard disk drive, your PC would be an empty shell with no memory and about as useful as a mobile phone on Mars. The hard disk drive is hidden away inside the case.

Floppy disk drive This drive uses cheap but low-capacity magnetic disks called, rather misleadingly, floppies. Floppy drives are now almost obsolete.

CD drive A CD drive can do one or more of these: read data from a pre-recorded compact *disc* (*CD-ROM*); save data onto a blank compact disc, but just once (*CD-R*); and save data onto a compact disc time and time again, overwriting existing data as required (*CD-RW*). A CD-RW drive can do all three.

DVD drive Now virtually standard equipment on new computers. DVD discs have a far greater capacity than CDs, which makes them ideal for distributing huge volumes of data. Your DVD drive can also play *DVD movies* and, if it's a DVD recorder, save files

Although an optional extra, a scanner is useful for turning paper-based documents and images into computer files.

onto blank DVD discs just like a CD-RW drive. If your computer has just one drive, chances are it's a CD/DVD 'combo' drive that combines all the functions of a CD-RW and a DVD recorder drive in a single unit.

Memory card reader This is not strictly a drive at all, but you may well find what looks like a drive with several horizontal slots built into the system unit. This is a memory card reader. You use it to copy files to and from memory cards used in digital cameras and music players.

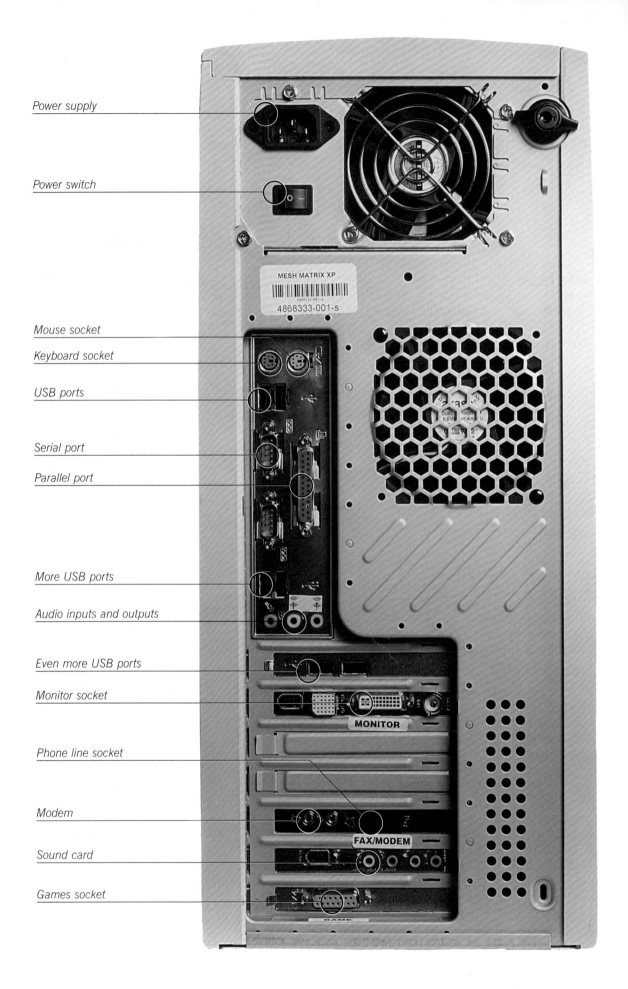

Power supply

Power switch

MESH MATRIX XP

4868333-001-s

Mouse socket

Keyboard socket

USB ports

Serial port

Parallel port

More USB ports

Audio inputs and outputs

Even more USB ports

Monitor socket

MONITOR

Phone line socket

Modem

FAX/MODEM

Sound card

Games socket

Ethernet is a standard used for connecting computers in a network.

Windows XP Home Edition.

Interfaces

It's time to look around the back. Scary stuff? Not a bit of it. First off, near the top, you'll find a large three-pin socket for connecting the power supply and possibly a power switch. Once you've connected the power cable and flicked the power switch to the on position, you shouldn't need to bother with these again.

Just about everything else is an *interface* of some sort – that is, a port or socket used to connect other hardware devices to the system unit. In fact, there are two types of interfaces: integrated and expansion cards. Okay, this is getting just a little jargony but bear with us for a moment.

Integrated interfaces are permanently soldered to the motherboard. In this example, we see sockets for the mouse and keyboard, four *USB* ports, two *serial* ports one *parallel* port, and a bunch of audio inputs and outputs. Your computer will also have an *Ethernet* port, with which it can connect to other computers in a *network*.

Lower down the case, we find several other input and output interfaces grouped together in rows. These are expansion cards. An expansion card is simply a circuit board that plugs in to the internal motherboard. Each is dedicated to a particular function or range of related duties. The main attraction of expansion cards is that they can be easily removed and replaced, which adds flexibility and expansion possibilities to your PC.

Topmost is yet another pair of USB ports. Below these we find the *video card*. This expansion card is responsible for producing the pictures you see on your monitor screen. The monitor plugs in here.

The next two slots are currently covered by metal 'blanking plates' but these could be easily removed from within if we wanted to install new expansion cards.

Below them is the *modem*, essential for connecting your computer to the internet. One socket is used to connect the modem to the telephone line; the other lets you connect a telephone handset.

The next expansion card is the *sound card*, to which you connect speakers and, optionally, headphones, a microphone or pretty much any external sound source. The sound card, you see, is just as well equipped to record sound as it is to play music and make other noises.

Finally, we find a games socket, used to connect a joystick or other controller when playing computer games. You could also connect a *MIDI* instrument here to record your own music. The games socket is usually found on the sound card itself but in this case there simply wasn't room and so it has been given a slot all of its own.

Software

Software is any set of coded instructions that a computer can understand. When you press a key on the keyboard, the computer knows that something has happened; however, it takes software to turn the raw electronic signal into an instruction to display, say, the letter Q. We'll look at software in detail later but for now let's concentrate on an absolutely critical trichotomy that baffles even many experienced computer owners: the difference between the operating system, application software and driver software.

Operating system A multi-faceted software program that runs the computer. In the present case, this is a program developed by Microsoft called Windows XP Home Edition. Windows is a graphical program, which means you interact with it by means of on-screen objects and *menus* i.e. you don't have to learn a complex language of text commands. This makes computers easy to use. It does not, however, make them entirely intuitive, which is why we've written this manual.

From now on, we will refer to the operating system simply as Windows.

Application software Although an operating system like Windows contains many useful programs that go well beyond the basics of running the computer, it is not by itself sufficient to make a PC practical in the long term. For this you need application software i.e. dedicated programs designed for specific tasks. You need application software to write a letter, surf the internet or play around with *digital* pictures.

From now on, we will refer to application software simply as programs.

Driver software Special code that enables a computer to interact with hardware devices. When you buy, for instance, a new scanner, you will find two types of software in the box: application software, with which to edit scanned images, but also – and more importantly – driver software. The driver tells the computer that a scanner has just been bolted on to the system, that it's this particular make and model of scanner, and that it's capable of doing X, Y and Z. Without a driver sitting between the device and the operating system, nothing happens.

From now on, we will refer to the driver software simply as drivers.

All clear? Windows runs your computer, programs let you do interesting things with it, and drivers make your hardware work.

PART 1

Preparing your workstation

Your very first task before unpacking a thing should be deciding where to put it all. Computer equipment is heavy, fragile and a pain to shift from here to there, so let's plan it properly from the outset. We'll assume here that your computer system comprises a system unit, monitor, keyboard, mouse, speakers, printer and scanner. That's pretty much the norm these days.

Workstation or desk?

Workstations come in many shapes and sizes, from corner-hugging, space-saving, vertically-stacking units to great, sprawling, semi-permanent installations. The choice is yours, but we would caution against underestimating how much room your computer needs. Even with everything tucked away, you'll still need sufficient space to site your keyboard directly in front of the monitor with a mouse mat alongside. What about the speakers? The printer and scanner? A telephone? Will you still be able to lay out documents as you work on them? Factor in a little personal elbow room, too: you will, after all, spend a good deal of time with your computer (no, really, you will).

The main attraction of a purpose-built workstation is that you can find one to fit any available space. But don't be tempted to splash out if you have a perfectly serviceable desk to hand.

Support your wrists with a gel-filled rest.

Power points

Your computer system is going to require five plug sockets: one each for the system unit, monitor, speakers, printer and scanner. We would also suggest that you invest in a desk lamp, which makes it six. Invest in one or two of those power strip extensions with multiple sockets, and check that they comfortably extend to the rear of your workstation or desk. Moreover, only buy power strips with 'surge protection' built in. This will protect your valuable equipment if the electricity supply is subject to any fluctuations, such as those caused by heavy electrical equipment on the same mains circuit.

You might also consider an 'uninterruptible power supply' (i.e. a battery-powered unit that sits between your computer and the mains power and temporarily takes over in the event of a power cut).

To use the internet, you will need access to a telephone socket (see part 4). It might be worthwhile getting your telephone company to install a fresh socket behind your workstation, or perhaps installing an extension yourself. Failing that, plan how you will connect the back-end of your computer to the nearest socket. Trailing a cable across the carpet, under doors and up the stairs is not conducive to domestic harmony.

Also consider nearby sources of heat and light. Your computer will thank you not to be sited too close to a radiator, and you must allow it adequate ventilation (i.e. at least 30cm of clear space around the rear of the system unit and the monitor vents). Sit directly facing a window and you'll spend all summer squinting at the screen; sit with a window behind you and the screen will reflect the light back into your eyes. Your monitor generates its own bright images without the need for any external lighting so do your eyes a favour and avoid screen glare, even if it means compromising on the ideal site for your computer.

Invest in a fully-adjustable chair to save yourself from backache. A three-legged Chippendale copy liberated from the dining room really isn't up to the job.

Are you sitting comfortably?

Ergonomics, or the study of workplace design, is more a case of common sense than hard science. When arranging your workstation, there are two main considerations: comfort and safety. By comfort, we mean that you shouldn't have to crick your neck to see the monitor, prop yourself up on cushions to use the keyboard or crawl under the desk to reach your computer's CD-ROM drive. By safety, however, we must consider the dangers of using a computer for prolonged periods. Chief amongst the hazards is Repetitive Strain Injury, or RSI, involving such unpleasant complaints as tenosynovitis, tendonitis and carpal tunnel syndrome. Regular breaks and stretching exercises are advisable during a long session at the desk but equally important is adopting a sensible posture. Above all, any discomfort is a sign of stress, so respect your body's signals and take action before it is too late. RSI is a debilitating and often agonising condition.

Good posture and careful planning help avoid RSI.

Good posture begins with a straight back. A decent chair is essential but equally so is a cast-iron resolution not to hunch over your keyboard or slump in your seat.

When using the keyboard, your forearms should be horizontal and held at approximately 90° to your upper arms.

The back and the seat of your chair should both be adjustable for height and tilt. Adjustable arm rests are a good idea, and the chair should be absolutely stable. A five-legged platform is more stable than a three-legged one.

The top of your monitor screen should be no higher than eye level. Indeed, some research suggests that the monitor should ideally be positioned between 15° and 50° below eye level, much like you would hold a magazine. The screen should be at least 60cm away from your face.

Position the monitor directly in front of you, not offset to one side.

Your feet should be flat on the floor and your thighs horizontal or, preferably, tilted slightly forwards. Use a foot rest if necessary (no, not your scanner) to maintain a 90° angle between the thighs and shins. This helps support your back.

PART ① Plugging it all together

Here comes the daunting part – unpacking your new PC system and making it work. We'll assume that you've already sneaked a peep inside the boxes and panicked at the sight of endless CD-ROMs, manuals and cables. How on earth are you supposed to know where to start?

Get organised

First things first: let's unpack. Your computer system will be packed in several boxes, typically one each for the monitor, speakers, printer and scanner, and a further carton containing the system unit, keyboard, mouse and various bits and pieces. Carefully take everything out, lay it out on the floor and check it against the delivery paperwork. This may be easier said than done, of course – you may not appreciate (or particularly care) that 'ATI RADEON 8500 64MB DV (ALL IN WONDER)' refers to the computer's internal video card, so simply keep an eye open for obvious omissions. If there's no monitor, get on the blower.

Here is a list of everything delivered with our system:

- One computer in a tower system unit
- One monitor with manual
- One keyboard
- One *5.1* speaker system with cables, power supply and set-up guide
- One large, clearly illustrated and very welcome installation sheet
- One printer
- One scanner

'It'll be nice when it's finished,' you muse hopefully when confronted with boxes of unconnected hardware. And you're right . . . it will be.

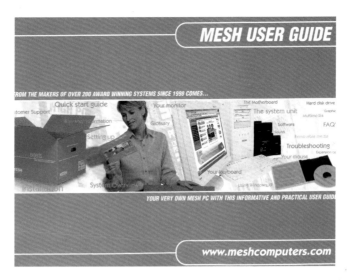

Well, you've already got this manual so you may not need the one that comes with your computer. But keep it safe just in case.

So far, so obvious. But then we came upon this little lot:

User guide The main manual! Very important.

Customer support guide Equally important. This tells you how to get technical help.

Two three-pin power cables One each for the system unit and the monitor.

Modem cable Connects the PC's modem to the phone socket.

Monitor adaptor This little adaptor means that we can connect an older-style CRT monitor to the modern *DVI* interface on the video card.

Video card manual You may need to refer to the manual to understand the video card's features.

Motherboard manual If you ever open up your computer to perform an upgrade, this manual will prove invaluable. Until then, keep it safe and don't give it another thought.

Modem manual This will come in useful later when we set up our internet connection.

Windows XP recovery CD-ROM This can get you out of trouble if your PC starts to experience severe problems.

Sound card CD-ROM This disc contains the drivers necessary to get the sound card working. However, most computer manufacturers pre-install essential software so that your computer works 'straight out of the box'. This disc would only be required if you ever had to re-install the sound card.

Video card CD-ROM Ditto.

Modem CD-ROM Ditto.

Video-editing CD-ROM Programs for editing video footage on the PC.

CD/DVD-burning CD-ROM Programs for recording data, audio or video compilations onto blank CD and DVD discs.

Office suite CD-ROM Programs for writing letters, keeping records and doing all sorts of creative things like that. You may have been supplied with an armful of application software – or none at all.

Mouse mat A mat for the mouse.

Oh, and the mouse The mouse itself.

Phew! Little wonder people panic.

A monitor adaptor lets you connect an older-style CRT (big, bulky, cheap) monitor to a DVI video card designed for digital LCD (flat, lightweight, more expensive) monitors.

Laying it out

Set up the key components – system unit, monitor, keyboard and mouse – roughly as you plan to use them. Don't worry about the cables and wiring; everything can hang loose for now.

If you've acquired an older-style CRT monitor, which would only be the case if you bought your system second-hand, you will probably have to attach a swivel base to its underside first. This is usually straightforward, but start as you mean to go on and consult the monitor manual.

Now have a seat and see if it all feels just about right. Pay particular attention to any sources of glare on the monitor screen. Take the time now to make any adjustments, even if it means moving your workstation across the room or rethinking your power source. It's a good deal easier doing this now than after having made all the hardware connections.

Now bring the printer and scanner into play. Don't worry yet about any tape or security packing on these devices; simply take them from their boxes and make sure they fit their allotted space. In particular, remember that your printer will need to have input and output trays bolted on, which significantly increases its working area.

Finally, unpack and arrange your speakers. This could involve anywhere from two simple stereo speakers to four or five speakers if you opted for a 4.1 or 5.1 *'surround sound'* system. Or, indeed, no speakers at all if they are integrated within the monitor.

Unpack the smaller satellite speakers, attach any stands supplied and note the length of their cables. You should find that two speakers (or three in a 5.1 system) come with relatively short cables, perhaps a couple of metres each. Two others will have longer cables, typically five metres. One speaker with a short cable should be positioned either side of the monitor, equidistant from your seated position but with as much space between them as possible. The third short-cabled speaker (5.1 system only) should be sited as centrally as possible, perhaps on a shelf above the monitor or indeed perched on the monitor itself. In truth, only a true audiophile would object if you tucked it in to one side of the monitor.

The speakers with longer cables should now be located either side of and behind your seated position for the full surround sound effect.

At this point it's quite possible that all the computer salesman's patter about DVD movie soundtracks stunningly rendered in surround sound Dolby Digital will pale into insignificance when you realise that, in fact, there's just no convenient way to locate these satellites in your living room. If so, now is the time to cut your losses and settle for simple stereo sound, in which case you don't need the rear or central satellites at all.

With or without rear speakers, you will certainly want to use a *subwoofer* if one was supplied. This is a large, powerful unit that broadcasts deep bass tones. It should be located at floor level but needn't be centrally positioned (i.e. you don't have to stick it between your feet).

Arrange your hardware as you intend to use it before making connections.

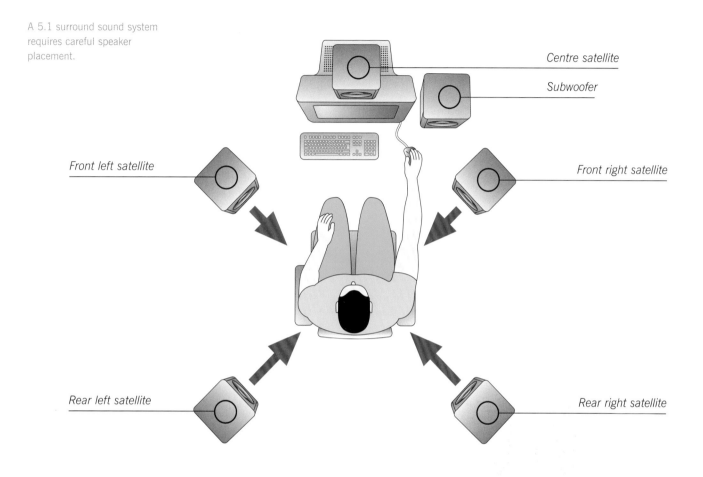

A 5.1 surround sound system requires careful speaker placement.

Centre satellite

Subwoofer

Front left satellite

Front right satellite

Rear left satellite

Rear right satellite

Once more, with everything roughly in place, satisfy yourself with your workstation arrangement.

Making connections

It's time to turn all this raw hardware into a working computer.

As we have already seen, the rear of the system unit hosts a range of electronic interfaces, each of which lets you connect a device to the system. Right now, you need to identify four, namely:

Monitor. This is either a blue *analogue* socket (*VGA*) for use with older-style CRT monitors or a white digital socket (DVI) for use with digital *LCD* monitors.

Just to confuse the issue, here we have to connect a CRT monitor to a DVI socket, hence the presence of the adaptor plug we unearthed earlier. In most cases, however, the thick white cable hard-wired to the monitor plugs straight into a VGA or DVI socket.

Keyboard. A round socket, usually colour-coded purple. The connector on the keyboard's cable is coloured correspondingly. How handy is that? Alternatively the keyboard may come with a USB connection.

Mouse. A similar story to the keyboard, but in green. Or in USB flavour.

Speakers. If you have simple stereo speakers, they will connect directly to the sound card in the system unit. However, in a surround sound system, the speakers do not connect to the sound card directly; rather, they connect to the subwoofer, which then connects to the sound card. Inevitably, all this plugging together of speakers involves a good deal of crawling around at floor level, which is why once again we exhort you to be sure that you're happy with your workstation before you make a start.

When you have identified these essentials, you can start to hook it all together.

Fancy speakers require fancy connections. Here, the five satellite speakers all plug into the subwoofer, and then the subwoofer hooks up to the system unit.

Begin with the monitor. Note how the shaped connector on the monitor cable fits the PC's socket in only one direction. Line them up and gently push the connector home, taking great care not to force it or bend the pins. Now secure the cable in position with the connector's integrated screws. Do NOT over-tighten them – the idea is merely to ensure that the connector will not slip or be easily knocked out of its socket. In this case, we are using the adaptor described above.

Now connect the keyboard and mouse. Note again that the pins on the connector and the holes in the socket must be carefully aligned. Follow the colour coding or look for descriptive stickers on the case next to the sockets – or, if you've a USB keyboard and/or mouse, simply plug them into any USB ports. Place the keyboard directly in front of the monitor on your desktop and the mouse on its mat to either the right or the left depending upon whether you're right- or left-handed.

The precise method for wiring up the speaker system depends upon your equipment but you will have been supplied with a guide. In this case, we have five satellite speakers to connect to the subwoofer. The subwoofer then connects to the sound card by means of three 3.5mm audio jacks. Take the time to ensure that each speaker is connected to the correct channel on the subwoofer (e.g. the speaker that sits to the left of the monitor on your workstation should be connected to the channel marked 'front left').

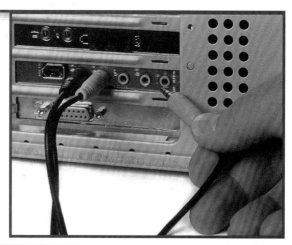

Connect the three-pin power cables to the system unit and monitor and plug them into the power strip. If the PC's power supply unit has a voltage selector, take a second to check that it is set correctly for your country (e.g. 240V in the UK). The PC's power supply unit may also have an on-off switch; if so, flick it to the on position now. Also plug the subwoofer into the power strip. Look for a power switch or button on the subwoofer case and turn it on. Volume controls should be set about a third of the way between minimum and maximum.

And that's that. Just to refresh:

- The monitor should be connected to the system unit's video card.
- The keyboard and mouse should be connected to the system unit.
- The satellite speakers should be connected to the subwoofer.
- The subwoofer should be connected to the system unit's sound card.
- The system unit, monitor and subwoofer should all be plugged into a surge-protected power strip.

Now plug the power strip into the mains electricity and flick the switch. Ready for some action? Turn to the next section.

Turning on for the first time ... and off again

Caller: 'Hello, technical support? I need help! My computer won't work properly.'

Technical Support: 'Hmm. Have you tried booting it?'

Caller: 'Hold on ...'

A sickening crunch is heard

Caller: 'No, that didn't seem to help.'

Your first encounter with Windows Desktop and that all-important Start button.

Boot camp

To 'boot' (or 'power-up') a computer is to switch it on, so let's do just that. Shuffle your computer system back into the right arrangement on your workstation – everything may have moved about when you made the connections – and take a seat at your workstation.

It's good practice to turn on the monitor first because it means you can read any messages that appear on screen. Do this now. There's usually a biggish button on the front, but check the manual if you're not certain.

Now push the larger button on the front of the system unit. Hear that whirring sound? That's the internal cooling fans springing into action, without which your computer would melt. Watch the screen and you'll likely see some gobbledegook in white letters on a black background. That's fine; ignore it. Soon, you will see a Windows welcome screen followed quickly by the Windows Desktop. You will even hear a congratulatory tune tinkle forth from your speakers. This is Windows saying hello.

Exactly what you see at this point depends upon how your computer manufacturer has set up your system, but as long as there's a green button labelled 'start' in the lower left corner of the screen – hereafter referred to as the Start *button* – you've made it. This is the Desktop. Windows XP is up and running and ready for action.

The great escape

Here's an oddity: the very first thing you should do having turned on your computer is turn it straight back off again. This is because it is very, very important to learn the correct approach and follow it every time. Here's another oddity: switching off begins with the Start button.

We're going to practise using the mouse shortly, so for now you may not find the following steps natural or easy. But just take your time and you'll get there (well, hopefully – now might be a good time to forget all about that client mentioned in the introduction).

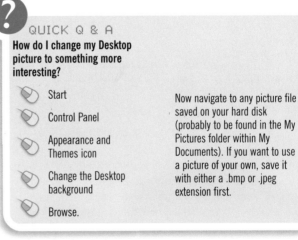

QUICK Q & A

How do I change my Desktop picture to something more interesting?

- Start
- Control Panel
- Appearance and Themes icon
- Change the Desktop background
- Browse.

Now navigate to any picture file saved on your hard disk (probably to be found in the My Pictures folder within My Documents). If you want to use a picture of your own, save it with either a .bmp or .jpeg extension first.

➊

Start

When you move the mouse around on its mat, the onscreen pointer matches its movements. Push the mouse forwards (i.e. towards the back of your desk) and the pointer moves up the screen; slide it to the right and the pointer follows suit. Your task is to make the pointer point at the Start button in the lower left corner of the screen. When it's in position, press and release the left mouse button with your index finger. This is called clicking. If the mouse jerks out of position at this point, just use your other hand to keep it steady and persevere. Don't worry, this will all become second-nature soon enough!

➋

Turn Off Computer

When you make a successful 'click', a menu will pop up above the Start button. Right at the bottom, you'll see a red button labelled Turn Off Computer. Move the mouse until the pointer points straight at this button, and click it once again.

➌

Turn Off Computer

Up pops a box with three buttons: Stand By, Turn Off and Restart. This time, make the pointer point at the middle button, Turn Off, and click the left mouse button again. Windows will now shut itself down. It may also switch off the system unit and perhaps even the monitor. If not, you'll see a message telling you that it's safe to turn off your computer. This is your cue to push the power switch on the system unit case to kill the power. Turn off the monitor, too.

Turn off computer

Stand By   Turn Off   Restart

Cancel

Restart

If you click Restart instead of Turn Off, your computer will turn itself off and then immediately back on again. This is useful in two main circumstances: either because you have to restart your computer before new software will work, or because you have some problem – such as a 'frozen' program – and you want to make a fresh start. Restarting your computer is the easiest way out of all sorts of difficulties.

But sometimes a frozen program or other bug means you can't actually use the Restart option. You'll find that you click the Start button but nothing happens. In this case, the first thing to do is leave your computer alone for a few minutes, just in case it manages to work out its problems all by itself. Failing that, press three keys simultaneously: Control, Alt and Delete. This should – and we emphasise should – produce a pop-up window called Windows Task Manager. Click the Shut Down menu option and select either Turn Off or Restart.

If even this does not work and your computer is completely 'stuck', there's nothing for it but to use the reset switch on the front of the system unit (sometimes you have to press and hold the main on/off power switch for a few seconds instead). This will cut power to the computer and then restart it. All problems should be over.

Stand By

This option doesn't quite switch your computer off or restart it. Rather, it switches to a lower power state where it's still technically running but the screen goes blank and you can't do anything. Any open windows and programs will remain open and you can return to full operation at any time just by pressing a key on the keyboard

or clicking the mouse. Stand By mode is really designed for laptops where power consumption is a critical factor. On a desktop system, it's hard to see a use for it, other than that it's a convenient way of leaving open tasks running while you go off and do something else or go to bed. However, for that you really want hibernation…

Hibernate

This option does switch off your computer completely but first it saves a record of what you are currently doing. Let's say you have a letter open in a word processor and a song playing in your music player. If you select the Hibernate option, Windows effectively freezes the moment. When you come back to the computer and turn it on again, you'll find yourself exactly where you left off. Your letter will still be open and your song will restart. Hibernate is a great option when you're in the middle of a project that you'll want to resume later.

Importantly, Stand By doesn't save this record so if there was a power outage during Stand By mode, you would lose any unsaved work. With Hibernate, everything is saved to the hard disk first so you could still pick up where you left off even after a power outage.

But where is this elusive Hibernate button? For reasons unknown, it does not appear by default on the Turn off computer menu. To access it, press the Shift key (see p.42) on the keyboard when the Turn off computer menu is on screen. You'll find that the Stand By button becomes Hibernate. Click it to put your computer in hibernation.

If this doesn't work, you may need to activate Hibernate on your computer first. Click Start, then Control Panel, then Performance and Maintenance, and finally Power Options. Now look for a tab (a tab is a page within a menu) called Hibernate. Click the tab and ensure that the box labelled Enable hibernation has a tick in it. If not, click inside this box and the tick will appear. Click Apply followed by OK to make the change and close the open windows. Now click the Start button again and click Turn Off Computer. This time, Hibernate should appear on the menu when you press the Shift key.

QUICK Q & A

Why does Windows ask me to 'activate' it?

When you first turn on your computer, you may well find a prompt asking you to activate your copy of Windows. This procedure tells Microsoft that you have a genuine copy of Windows, not a pirate copy. We suggest that you select the 'activate later' option until you have set up your internet connection. Don't worry – you'll be prompted to activate time and time again for the next 30 days so there's no hurry!

Log Off

This option is most useful when you have multiple 'user accounts' set up on your computer. We'll come to it in Appendix 3.

PART **2**

First steps

OK, so you've set up your computer and turned it on and off. Our guess is that you're itching to do something *useful* with it … but we're going to crave your indulgence and ask you to hang fire a while longer. These next few pages are absolutely critical: if you can master mouse and keyboard control right from the outset, even at the most basic level, all that follows will be so much easier.

We'll also get your printer and scanner up and running in this section.

PART ② Make friends with your mouse

A natural extension of your hand, or a slippery lump of plastic that slides around out of control and drives you to distraction? Like it or loathe it, the mouse is such an integral part of modern computing that nothing pays dividends like mastering it early.

Anatomy of a mouse

Windows is a graphical operating system for your computer, which means that you get to work with pictures and other visual clues instead of having to type text commands (as in the *bad old days*). The mouse enables you to interact with these graphics.

As in Part 1, you can see this by moving the mouse on its mat while Windows is running – every motion is replicated by the onscreen pointer.

Hardware-wise, the average modern mouse has two buttons with a wheel lodged between them. The left button is the primary button – i.e. it is used most frequently and performs most common tasks – while the right button generally invokes special shortcuts. The wheel, if present, can have a number of functions but is mainly used to 'scroll' through long documents and *web pages*.

Some mice have an integrated rubber ball on their undersides and work best on hard rubber mouse mats that help the ball rotate freely and accurately. Others, called optical mice, use a light instead of a ball and work on just about any surface. With an optical mouse, you don't need a mouse mat as it should work just fine directly on your desk or workstation. The exception is if you have a glass-covered surface, on which a mouse mat is a must.

Hold your mouse gently but firmly as shown below with your index and middle fingers resting lightly on the buttons. Practise just sliding it around the mat for a while and watch the onscreen pointer mimic its movements. It's very relaxing. Unfortunately, it doesn't get you very far.

The mouse pointer is an onscreen arrow controlled by your mouse. Use it to, er, point at things, and click them.

There's no need to squeeze the life out of your mouse – hold it gently, get your fingers in position and practise until it feels natural.

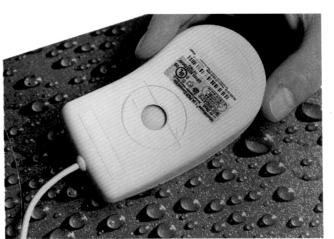

Keep your mouse free from fluff to keep it running smoothly.

Some funky things to do with a mouse

Here, then, are the key mouse concepts used in everyday home computing. Refer to the Conventions section on pages 8-9 for a refresher on the symbols used below.

Point-and-click. *This is where you make the onscreen pointer point at something, like an icon or a menu, and then press and release the left mouse button. It makes a satisfying clicking sound, hence the term 'click'. This is generally abbreviated to, for example, 'click the Start button'.*

 Start

 Start

Use the mouse to make the onscreen pointer point at the Start button in the bottom-left corner of your screen and click the left button once. This makes the Start Menu pop up. Now click the button again to make the menu disappear. What could be simpler?

Double-click. *Instead of pressing and releasing the mouse button once, here you click it twice in rapid succession. Why? Well, in certain circumstances, the first click merely '**selects**' the given object and the second click 'activates' it. Unless we specifically say 'double-click', assume that any direction refers to a single-click.*

 Clock

 Cancel

OK, this takes some explaining! Your computer's clock is tucked away in the very bottom-right corner of your screen. Point at the digits and click the left mouse button twice quickly. Up pops a window with lots of nice clock options, including a way to change the time. We don't want to do this, however, so click the Cancel button – a single-click this time – to make the window go away.

Don't fret if you struggle with this one, particularly if the mouse moves slightly between clicks or you don't manage to click quickly enough to launch the clock. We'll show you a way to make life easier in a moment. When you can launch and close the clock window with impunity, award yourself a well-earned Double-click Diploma.

31

3

Drag. *Another absolutely central mouse operation. Dragging involves a click-and-hold manoeuvre whereby you point at something, press the left mouse button and then keep the button depressed instead of releasing it straight away.*

 My Computer icon

Double-click the My Computer icon on the Desktop to open a window. Move the onscreen pointer to one edge of the window. See how it suddenly changes shape to a double-headed arrow? Now click and hold the left mouse button just as the pointer changes shape. Then, keeping the button depressed, move the double-headed arrow slightly to the left and slightly to the right. The window will expand and contract accordingly. When you release the mouse button, the window stays the way you leave it.

Also point at one of the windows corners and watch the pointer change shape to a slanted double-headed arrow. Now click, hold and drag in a diagonal direction. This resizes the window horizontally and vertically simultaneously.

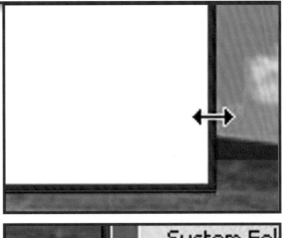

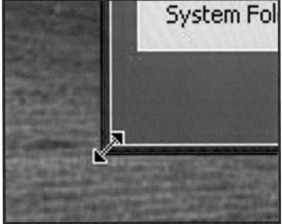

4

Drag-and-drop. *A closely related discipline that involves moving an object rather than resizing it. The initial technique is just the same.*

 My Computer icon

This time, point at the middle of the Title Bar i.e. the wide, coloured upper-edge of the window that tells you the name of the window – in this case, My Computer. The pointer will not change shape. Now click the left mouse button and, keeping the button depressed as before, drag the entire window up, down and all around the Desktop. See how it follows the movements of the mouse? At any time, you can release the mouse button to 'drop' the window in a new position. Again, close the window when you're through by clicking the small cross in the top-right corner.

Well, we're getting a little ahead of ourselves here, playing around with serious concepts like icons and windows before offering any real explanation as to what these things are and how they work. It's all a bit chicken and egg, really – it's important to be competent with the mouse and keyboard before tackling Windows but acquiring this competency inevitably involves using Windows. Still, not to worry. It is all good practice and will all make perfect sense soon enough.

Right-clicking

All computer mice have (at least) two buttons. Most of the time, you'll use the left button but we'd like to encourage you to experiment with the right button as well. Wherever you are – in Windows, using a program, browsing the web, writing an email – just take a second to click the right button and see what happens. Don't worry, you can't possibly do any harm: the right button invariably opens a menu with some options. What's important is that this menu is context-sensitive. That is, the menu options change according to where you are and what you're doing at the time. Here are some examples.

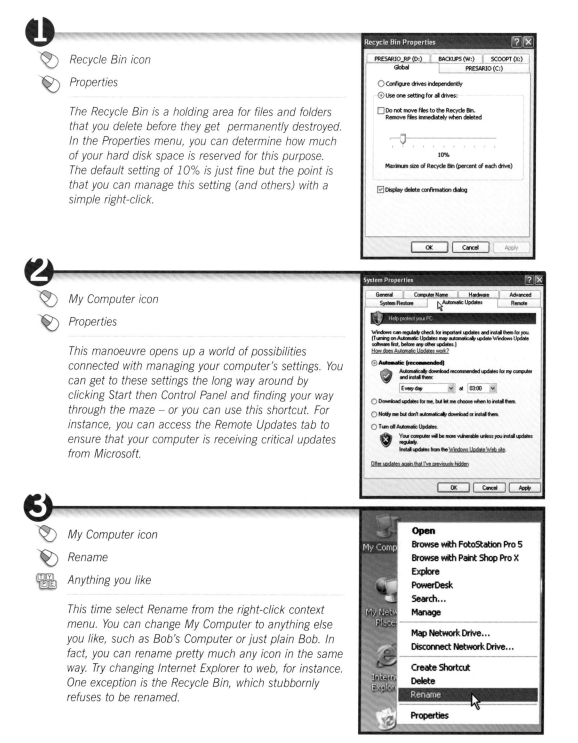

①

Recycle Bin icon

Properties

The Recycle Bin is a holding area for files and folders that you delete before they get permanently destroyed. In the Properties menu, you can determine how much of your hard disk space is reserved for this purpose. The default setting of 10% is just fine but the point is that you can manage this setting (and others) with a simple right-click.

②

My Computer icon

Properties

This manoeuvre opens up a world of possibilities connected with managing your computer's settings. You can get to these settings the long way around by clicking Start then Control Panel and finding your way through the maze – or you can use this shortcut. For instance, you can access the Remote Updates tab to ensure that your computer is receiving critical updates from Microsoft.

③

My Computer icon

Rename

Anything you like

This time select Rename from the right-click context menu. You can change My Computer to anything else you like, such as Bob's Computer or just plain Bob. In fact, you can rename pretty much any icon in the same way. Try changing Internet Explorer to web, for instance. One exception is the Recycle Bin, which stubbornly refuses to be renamed.

4

🖱 *Clock*

Let's say your computer is showing the wrong time. How do you adjust the clock? Well, you could spend an age trying to figure this out but instead try right-clicking it. Up pops a menu that includes this option: Adjust Date/Time. Again, a right-click gives you access to the most likely tools you need at the time.

5

🖱 *Desktop*

🖱 *New*

🖱 *Folder*

Right-click anywhere on the Desktop (don't worry if terms like Desktop are unfamiliar for now; we'll cover them in detail in Part 3). Now create a new folder using these simple steps. It will be called New Folder, which is less than useful. So now repeat step 3 and call it something meaningful like My Notes. You can create folders anywhere in Windows using this right-click route.

6

🖱 *New Folder icon*

🖱 *Delete*

🖱 *Yes*

Let's say you don't really want a new folder on your Desktop after all, or that you want to do away with any other folder or file. There are various ways to achieve this but the quickest is by right-clicking it and selecting Delete. Windows will ask you to confirm your intentions. The folder will then be moved to the Recycle Bin.

7

 Recycle Bin icon

🖱 *Empty Recycle Bin*

As we mentioned in Step 1, the Recycle Bin stores files and folders when you delete them, just in case you later want to get one back again. If you want to completely remove the Recycle Bin's entire contents, all you need is … yes, a right-click.

Incidentally, you can permanently delete any file or folder without going through the Recycle Bin holding stage. To do this, select the item you want to delete and hold down the Shift key while performing Step 6. That item will then be gone forever. Take care with this, as there's no way back.

Practice makes perfect

So much for the theory. But having already used the mouse to shut down your computer, you may be worried that you'll never get the hang of the thing. Here's an easy and fun way to practise. First, turn on your computer. Then do this:

1

🖱️ *Start*

🖱️ *All Programs*

🖱️ *Games*

🖱️ *Solitaire*

What we have here is Windows' own electronic version of the card game Solitaire, or Patience, and it's a great way to develop accurate mouse control. These directions obviously relate to one particular deal of the cards but just apply the general principles.

2

The Ace of any suit can be dragged to one of the vacant stacking areas above the main playing area. Here the Ace of Spades happens to be in column four. Point at the card, click and hold the left mouse button, then carefully drag the card to the leftmost stacking area. Now release the mouse button. Don't worry if you mess it up a few times, as the card will simply snap back to its original position on the 'table'.

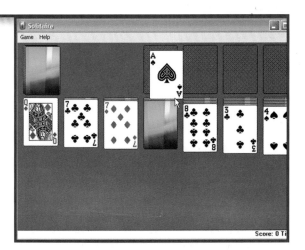

3

To move the red Seven onto the black Eight (or whatever), click on the card and drag-and-drop it into position i.e. release the mouse button when it's positioned roughly over the Eight of Clubs. You don't have to be too precise. See how it automatically snaps into place? Move as many cards as you can at this point.

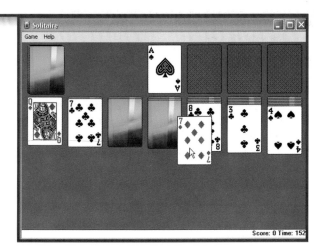

Now you need to flip over any newly-exposed cards. Point at each in turn and click once to turn it over. If this opens up new playing possibilities, drag and drop the cards as before. The Two of any suit may be dragged away from the main playing area and stacked on top of the relevant Ace in a stacking area, followed by the Three and the Four and so forth.

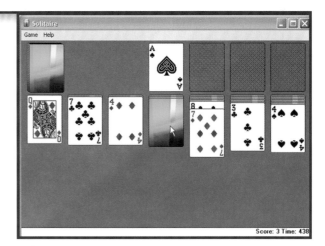

To deal some new cards three at a time, click the deck in the top-left corner. Drag-and-drop any suitable cards into the main playing area: in this case, the Ten of Hearts can go to the Jack of Clubs.

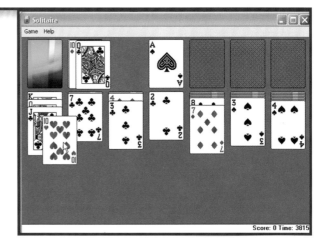

You can also drag a stack of cards from one column to another: in this case, the Eight of Clubs and the Seven of Diamonds from column five onto the Nine of Diamonds in column two. It's a little fiddly but the trick is to click onto the exposed upper-edge of the black Eight. The Seven remains locked to the Eight as you drag-and-drop the cards onto the red Nine.

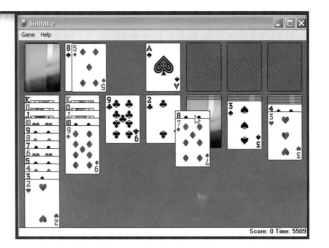

7

When the deck has been fully dealt, a circle appears in the now-empty dealing area. Click the circle once to make the remaining deck jump back to the dealing area, and click again to start the dealing afresh. Keep moving cards to the Ace stacks whenever possible and see if you can clear the entire playing area.

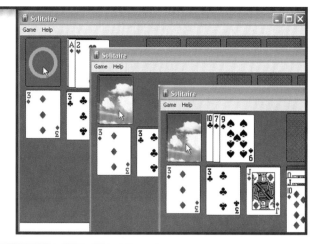

8

Game

Deal

At any time, you can begin a fresh game by clicking the Game button on the Toolbar above the playing area. When the dropdown menu appears, click Deal.

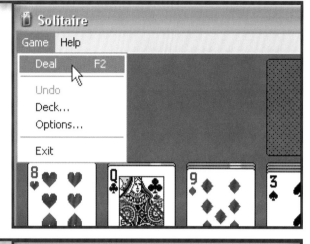

9

Help

Contents

Solitaire

Play Solitaire

*We're rather taking it for granted that you know how to play Solitaire! If not, consult the **Help menu**. This is excellent practice that will stand you in good stead when you come to work with more advanced application software later.*

Select any topic in the left window pane and instructions appear to the right. When you've read as far as you can, click-and-hold the scrollbar on the right edge of the window and drag it slowly towards the bottom of the window. This has the effect of 'scrolling' the instructions so you can read them all. Alternatively, click the small arrow buttons at the top and bottom of the scrollbar [see p. 74 for scrollbar details].

(You might also care to experiment with your mouse wheel at this point – roll it backwards and forwards to make the page scroll up and down.)

When you're finished, click the small, square cross button located at the very top-right corner of the Help

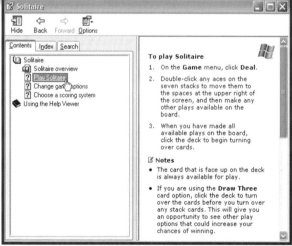

window. This closes the window and returns you to the game.

To close the Solitaire program itself, click the cross in the top-right corner of the window. There, it's as simple as that. Once you can comfortably drag-and-drop single or stacked cards from one column to another, deal from the deck and start a new game, you can truly say that you have mastered mouse control. What's more, you have learned a good deal about Windows (and windows) in the process without even trying!

Restraining the rodent

If, however, you really struggle with these practice exercises, there is a way to make the mouse more malleable. Proceed as follows:

1

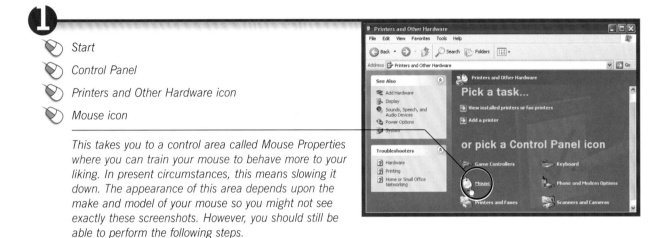

Start

Control Panel

Printers and Other Hardware icon

Mouse icon

This takes you to a control area called Mouse Properties where you can train your mouse to behave more to your liking. In present circumstances, this means slowing it down. The appearance of this area depends upon the make and model of your mouse so you might not see exactly these screenshots. However, you should still be able to perform the following steps.

2

Pointer Options

Open the Pointer Options tab. A tab works like a divider in a folder, separating the contents into similar subject matter. To open a tab and view its contents, simply point at the title and click once.

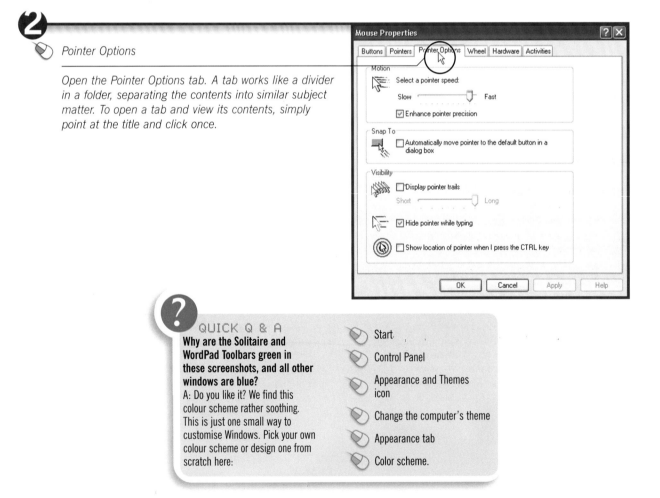

QUICK Q & A

Why are the Solitaire and WordPad Toolbars green in these screenshots, and all other windows are blue?

A: Do you like it? We find this colour scheme rather soothing. This is just one small way to customise Windows. Pick your own colour scheme or design one from scratch here:

Start

Control Panel

Appearance and Themes icon

Change the computer's theme

Appearance tab

Color scheme.

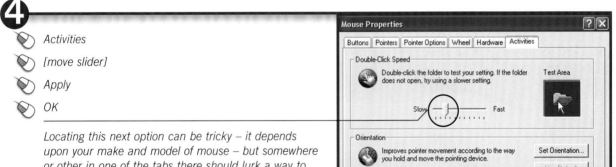

3

- [move slider]
- Apply

In the Motion area, you will see a graphical representation of a sliding scale. This relates to the sensitivity of the onscreen pointer in relation to your mouse (i.e. the closer the slider is to the Fast end of the spectrum, the faster the pointer travels across the screen). Click the slider control, drag it towards the left end of the scale, and release the mouse button just before it reaches Slow. Now slide the mouse around on its mat and note how you have to make big movements to move the pointer a small distance. If you like the effect, click the Apply button. If not, keep experimenting with the slider until you find a pointer speed that feels comfortable. Do not click the OK button until you have completed Step 4.

Mouse Properties

Buttons | Pointers | Pointer Options | Wheel | Hardware | Activities

Motion
Select a pointer speed:
Slow ——————— Fast
☑ Enhance pointer precision

Snap To
☐ Automatically move pointer to the default button in a dialog box

Visibility
☐ Display pointer trails
Short ——————— Long

☑ Hide pointer while typing

☐ Show location of pointer when I press the CTRL key

OK | Cancel | Apply | Help

4

- Activities
- [move slider]
- Apply
- OK

Locating this next option can be tricky – it depends upon your make and model of mouse – but somewhere or other in one of the tabs there should lurk a way to slow the mouse's double-click speed. Increasing the delay is ideal if you have trouble double-clicking quickly enough. In this example, we found the option in the Activities tab. Drag the slider to the Slow end of the scale. You should now be able to test your new setting by double-clicking a folder (or a jack-in-the-box, or something similar). Experiment until you can open the folder or spring the jack with a double-click every time, even if it means using the very slowest setting. Finally, click the Apply button to confirm the change, and then click OK to close the Mouse Properties window.

Mouse Properties

Buttons | Pointers | Pointer Options | Wheel | Hardware | Activities

Double-Click Speed
Double-click the folder to test your setting. If the folder does not open, try using a slower setting.
Test Area

Slow ——————— Fast

Orientation
Improves pointer movement according to the way you hold and move the pointing device.
Set Orientation...
Use Default

ClickLock
Enables you to highlight or drag without holding down the button. To set, briefly hold down the primary button. To release, click the button again.
☐ Turn on ClickLock
Settings...

Microsoft **IntelliPoint**

OK | Cancel | Apply | Help

PART  Get to grips with your keyboard

Having looked in some detail at the mouse, we now turn to the keyboard. Although it's actually possible to operate a computer entirely with the keyboard – that is, the keyboard can do anything the mouse can do, and more besides – in practice you'll use the mouse and keyboard in tandem. Certainly, until speech recognition technology comes of age (current forecast: 12 June 2179), you'll use it every time you need to write a letter or type a command.

Anatomy of a keyboard

Like the mouse, a keyboard is an input device (i.e. it lets you interact with your computer). On pages 42-43, we see a standard-issue-type keyboard with 102 keys (plus three special Windows-specific keys).

To use it, you press the keys lightly, either one at a time or occasionally in combinations of two or three. If a combination is called for – let's say [Ctrl] + [S] – this means that you press *and hold* the [Ctrl] key and then press the [S] key with [Ctrl] still depressed.

A good combination to practise – if only because it's as hard as it gets – is [Ctrl] + [Alt] + [Del]. You can achieve this in several ways but you'll certainly need both hands. Our favoured approach is pressing and holding [Ctrl] with the ring finger on the left hand, then pressing and holding [Alt] with the index finger on the same hand, and finally pressing [Del] with any finger at all on the right hand. This three-key combination summons the useful Windows Task Manager (see page 106). For now, however, simply press the [Esc] key to make it go away.

You may or may not wish to learn to touch-type. If so, there are plenty of software programs around that can help; or, of course, you could seek out a tutor. With instruction, you will learn how to position your hands correctly and which finger to use for each key. But quite frankly we couldn't give a hoot about any of that right now. Feel free to use your keyboard in any manner you choose, even if it means stabbing each key with a solitary digit or poking them with a pencil.

Guide to the main sections of a computer keyboard.

Alphanumeric keys. These are the familiar typewriter keys laid out in the standard QWERTY arrangement (this refers to the first six keys on the top line). Here we find all the letters of the alphabet, numbers 0–9 and the essential punctuation symbols.

Within and around this block, there are several important keys that take some further explaining.

Function keys. *Labelled* F1 *through to* F12*, these keys conjure up certain functions in certain programs. We won't be bothering with them but there's one useful shortcut you should know: in Windows, the* F1 *key acts as a shortcut to the Help & Support Centre.*

Spacebar. *This simply adds a space between words as you type.*

Esc. *The get-me-out-of-here-sharpish key. As a rule, the* Esc *key cancels the current operation or closes a dialogue box. Press one of the* Windows *keys to make the Start Menu pop up, and* Esc *to make it disappear again (yes, you've already done this back on page 31 but isn't it fun?).*

Tab. *Just like a typewriter, this indents paragraphs several spaces to the right.*

Caps Lock. *Press this key once and every letter key you type is printed in upper case; press it again to restore the keys to lower case. IF YOU LEAVE IT TURNED ON, YOUR TYPING WILL LOOK LIKE THIS.* Caps lock *is an example of a 'toggle' key – one press for on, another press for off.*

Shift. *You can also turn on upper case by pressing and holding this key as you type. Typically, you would capitalise the first letter of the first word in a sentence with the* Shift *key as it's quicker than turning the* Caps lock *function on and off again. The* Shift *key also lets you access the uppermost symbol on any key that has two possibilities. The number* 1 *key, for instance, prints an exclamation mark when you hold down* Shift*. Note that there are two* Shift *keys on your keyboard. They are entirely interchangeable.*

Ctrl. *Like the* Shift *key, this does nothing on its own but rather must be used in combination with other keys. For instance, pressing* Ctrl *and the letter* S *key together is a quick way of saving a document in most programs. There are two* Ctrl *keys.*

Windows. *Pressing the special* Windows *key, which is denoted by a flag, has the same effect as clicking the Start button. It also work as a combination key but we won't be calling upon its services. There are two* Windows *keys.*

Alt. *Yet another combination key that must be used in conjunction with other keys to have any effect. The second* Alt *key is actually called* Alt Gr*. We have absolutely no idea what it does and have never used it, so let's just give it a miss.*

Shift. *(see details bottom left)*

Backspace. *This key moves the cursor to the left one space at a time, and **deletes** any previous character. See the practical exercise with WordPad below for examples.*

Delete. *A key with many functions but in word processing it is generally used to erase the character immediately to the right of the current typing point. Again, we'll see how this works in a moment.*

Shortcut keys. *Many keyboards now feature an extra array of buttons that offer useful shortcuts e.g. launch an email program or web browser, navigate backwards and forwards through web pages, and adjust the speaker volume – all without touching the mouse. Nice to have but strictly non-essential.*

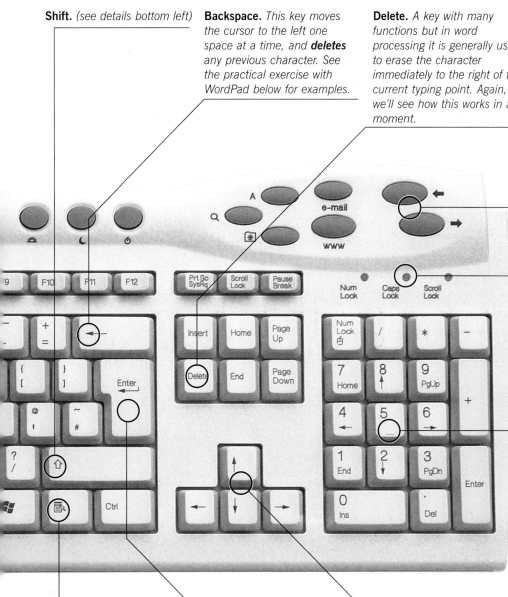

Lights. *Your keyboard also has three little status lights. One illuminates whenever the* Num lock *feature is active and another whenever* Caps lock *is on. The third relates to* Scroll lock *, a mysterious key that we have no knowledge of nor interest in.*

Numeric keypad. *With the keyboard's Num Lock function active (the **default** option when your computer starts; otherwise press* Num lock *) these calculator-style keys duplicate the number keys in the top row of the main section of the keyboard.*

With the Number Lock function disabled, the 2 *,* 4 *,* 6 *and* 8 *keys work just like a second set of arrow keys. The Home key takes you straight to the start of a line or the beginning of a web page; the End key takes you to the end. The Page Up/Page Down keys let you quickly scroll through an open document of web page on page, or screen, at a time.*

Shortcut. *This key has the same effect as clicking the right mouse button (see the explanation of right-clicking on [p33]).*

Enter. *This works primarily like the carriage return key on a traditional typewriter (i.e. starts a new line). There's a second* Enter *key tucked away at the very bottom-right corner of your keyboard. Also known as the Return key.*

Arrow keys. *This block of four arrows is primarily used to move the blinking cursor around the text on a printed page. What's a blinking cursor? Wait for [p.44].*

Practice makes perfect once again

OK, it's time to get a-clicking and put all this theory into practice. Again, we're going to jump the gun slightly and have you working with a Windows program, but just follow the directions closely and you'll have no difficulty. First, turn on your computer.

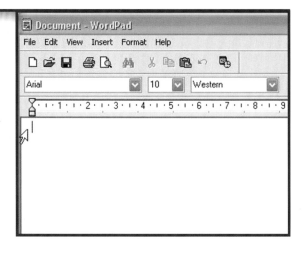

- Start
- All Programs
- Accessories
- WordPad

What we have here is the basic but functional word processor program that comes with Windows. You wouldn't write War and Peace with WordPad but it can certainly help you master your keyboard with some simple exercises.

First, click anywhere in the big white space. This, incidentally, is your computer's graphical representation of a sheet of paper. See that small vertical line blinking away in the top-left corner? This is technically known as the 'insertion point' because it's the point at which new text will be inserted, but we'll just call it the blinking cursor. Note that you still have a mouse pointer: just move the mouse around a bit and you'll see the familiar arrow dart around the screen. Confusing, isn't it? However, it's really important to recognise from the outset that these are quite distinct. The mouse pointer does what it always does – let's you control your computer – but the blinking cursor is contained within the page.

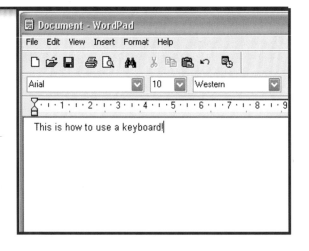

Press and hold down shift, press the letter T key, then release shift. There, you've just made a capital T. Now type H, I and S, and press the spacebar once. In our shorthand, this is:

[Shift] + [T]

[H] [I] [S] [Spacebar]

What you have here is a fully fledged word. Now continue as follows (just take it slow and steady):

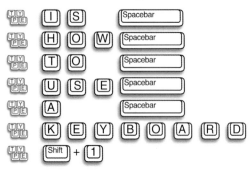

[I] [S] [Spacebar]

[H] [O] [W] [Spacebar]

[T] [O] [Spacebar]

[U] [S] [E] [Spacebar]

[A] [Spacebar]

[K] [E] [Y] [B] [O] [A] [R] [D]

[Shift] + [1]

3

If all went well, you should now be looking at this sentence in WordPad: 'This is how to use a keyboard!' Press [Enter] once, and note how the blinking cursor moves down to a fresh line. Press [Enter] again and it moves down the page still further. Now press [Backspace] twice to return the blinking cursor to the end of your sentence.

4

Experiment with the group of arrow keys. Each press of the [←] key moves the blinking cursor one character to the left. Keep pressing it until you reach the beginning of the first word. Now use the [→] to move the blinking cursor back through the text. This time, however, pause when the blinking cursor is just to the right of the letter 'o' in the word 'to'. Press the [Backspace] key twice to delete the word.
Now type [Shift] + [I].
Your sentences has changed to: 'This is how I use a keyboard!' That very simple edit shows the power of word processing.

5

This time, we want to change the word 'a' to 'my' but let's proceed slightly differently. Use the arrow keys to position the blinking cursor just to the left of the word 'a', then press [Del]. The effect is the same – you're deleting a word – but this time you've rubbed out characters to the right of the blinking cursor rather than to the left. Now press [M] followed by [Y].
Your sentence should now read: 'This is how I use my keyboard!' Keep practising with the arrow keys until you're comfortable positioning the blinking cursor anywhere within your sentence.

6

Move the blinking cursor to the right of the exclamation point and press [Enter] twice. Now type:

[1] [2] [3] [Enter]
[4] [5] [6] [Enter]
[7] [8] [9] [Enter]

You should now have three rows of three numbers. Use the arrow keys to move the blinking cursor to the left of number 4.

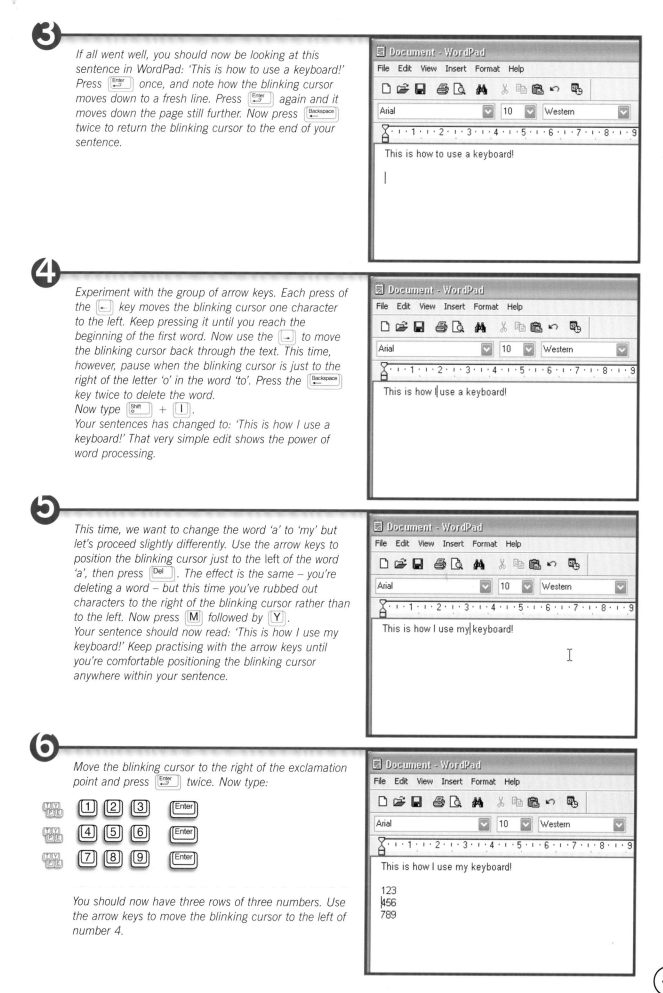

7

Now press the `Tab` key. This block of numbers will now be indented on the page. Move down to the beginning of the next block (i.e. to the left of number 7) and press `Tab` twice. This block will now be indented further. To remove the indents, position the blinking cursor just to the left of the numbers and use the `Backspace` key. Alternatively, position the blinking cursor at the very beginning of the line and use the `Del` key. This is simple formatting but already you can see how easy it is to arrange your words and numbers on a sheet of paper.

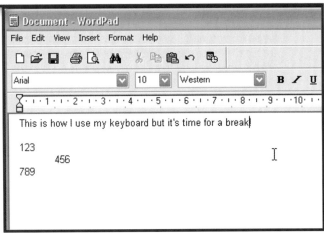

8

Finally, for now, return to your original sentence. Use the arrow keys to position the blinking cursor between the 'd' of 'keyboard' and the exclamation point. Now type:

TYPE `Spacebar` `B` `U` `T` `Spacebar`
TYPE `I` `T` `@/'` `S` `Spacebar`
TYPE `T` `I` `M` `E` `Spacebar`
TYPE `F` `O` `R` `Spacebar`
TYPE `A` `Spacebar`
TYPE `B` `R` `E` `A` `K`

Your new text is inserted straight into the original sentence, and everything to the right of the blinking cursor – in this case, just the explanation point – shuffles along to make space. You can't do that on a typewriter!

(Note that `@/'` is one of those dual function keys where a simultaneous press of the `Shift` key would have printed the @ character instead of an apostrophe.) Now go and make a cup of tea, but leave everything just as it is.

9

Ready for something a little fancier? You may have noticed that the mouse pointer changes shape depending on where in the window it happens to be. If you point at any of the buttons or menu options – File, Edit, View and so on – it looks like a normal pointer. However, if you move the pointer into the white page area, it changes to an 'I' shape. This is called an 'I-beam', and it offers an alternative way to manipulate text on the page.

10

Using the mouse, position the I-beam between the 'k' of 'break' and the exclamation point, and click once. The blinking cursor now moves to this position on the page. Don't worry if you miss a few times – just keep trying. If at any time the text becomes accidentally 'highlighted' (see Step 12 below), click on a blank spot on the page away from the text and the highlighting will disappear. Some people find the I-beam an easier way to position the blinking cursor within text than the arrow keys; others prefer the keyboard. Either way, you now have a choice.

Document - WordPad

File Edit View Insert Format Help

Arial | 10 | Western | **B** *I* <u>U</u>

This is how I use my keyboard but it's time for a break!

123
         456
789

11

Now move the mouse pointer to the beginning of your sentence and watch how it changes. As it approaches the first letter of the first word, it maintains an I-beam shape – but when you position it just to the left of the first word, it takes on the shape of an arrow. In contrast to the standard mouse pointer arrow, however, this arrow points to the right rather than to the left. What you have here is a 'selection tool'.

Document - WordPad

File Edit View Insert Format Help

Arial | 10 | Western | **B** *I* <u>U</u>

This is how I use my keyboard but it's time for a break!

12

To see it in action, click once just as the mouse pointer turns from an I-beam into the selection tool. As if by magic, the entire line of text that it's pointing at becomes highlighted. This means that you can treat that text as a single unit and 'process' it in any way you choose. You might drag the sentence from one part of the page to another, for example, or change the font size or colour.

Document - WordPad

File Edit View Insert Format Help

Arial | 10 | Western | **B** *I* <u>U</u>

This is how I use my keyboard but it's time for a break!

13

But for now, let's just delete our text. With the text highlighted, press the [Del] key. Now highlight any remaining text or numbers line-by-line with the selection tool and delete the lot until you have a blank page. Finally, close WordPad by clicking the cross in the top-right corner of the window. The program will ask you if you want to save changes to the document. Click the No button.

WordPad

⚠ Save changes to Document?

Yes   No   Cancel

Sedating the keyboard

The thing that most people find trickiest about the keyboard is pressing and releasing the keys quickly enough. If you hold down a key for fractionally too long, the character is repeated on the pageeee (oops, there's an extra e or three right there). Having tried the exercises above, you'll know whether this applies to you. If so, here's how to make life a little easier. Proceed as follows:

Start

Control Panel

Printers and Other Hardware icon

Keyboard icon

This takes you to a control area called Keyboard Properties. The appearance of this area depends upon the make and model of your keyboard so you might not see exactly these screenshots. However, you should still be able to perform the following steps.

Speed

Open the Speed tab, or look in each tab until you find a section called Character Repeat. As a reminder, a tab is like a divider in a folder, separating the contents into related groups. To select a tab, simply point at the title – in this case Speed – and click once.

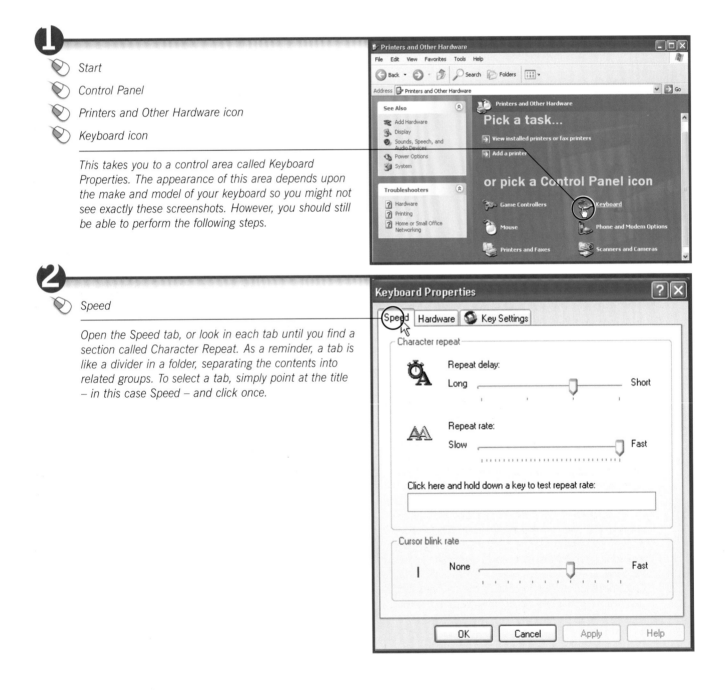

❸

🔤 *[test repeat rate]*

Within the Character Repeat section, you will find a testing area that looks like a white rectangle. Point at this with mouse pointer and click once. A blinking cursor will appear within the box. This is your cue to start typing. Type any word or phrase and note how quickly a character repeats when you don't release the key quickly enough. If you run out of space, use the Backspace key to delete your text.

Keyboard Properties [?][X]

Speed | Hardware | 🔄 Key Settings

Character repeat

Ȁ̈ Repeat delay:
Long ———————▢——— Short

Ȁ̈ Repeat rate:
Slow —————————▢ Fast

Click here and hold down a key to test repeat rate:

tte;tinggg

Cursor blink rate

None ——————▢———— Fast

[OK] [Cancel] [Apply] [Help]

❹

🖱️ *[move Repeat Delay slider]*

🖱️ *[move Repeat Rate slider]*

🖱️ *Apply*

🖱️ *OK*

If you find that your natural typing speed is too slow and extraneous letters keep appearing, you have two options. Repeat Delay governs how quickly a second character is printed after a key is pressed. The longer the delay, the less the chance of unwanted repeat characters. Repeat Rate determines how quickly subsequent characters then appear. The slower the rate, the fewer unwanted repeat characters. So, click-and-hold the slider controls in turn and move Repeat Delay to the Long end of the spectrum and Repeat Rate to Slow. Click anywhere in the test box again and you should find that your keyboard is now much more forgiving.
Click the Apply button to confirm the changes, and then click OK to close the Keyboard Properties window.

Keyboard Properties [?][X]

Speed | Hardware | 🔄 Key Settings

Character repeat

Ȁ̈ Repeat delay:
Long ▢——————————— Short

Ȁ̈ Repeat rate:
Slow ——▢—————————— Fast

Click here and hold down a key to test repeat rate:

ttestinggg

Cursor blink rate

None ——————▢———— Fast

[OK] [Cancel] [Apply] [Help]

PART 2 Connecting the printer

It won't have escaped your notice that a couple of hunks of hardware are currently lying dormant on your desk or workstation. But now that you've had some practice with the mouse, keyboard and Windows itself, it's time to hook up the printer.

No two printers share exactly the same setup routine so you may have to interpret the following pictures and directions to suit. In particular, if you have opted for a laser printer rather than an inkjet, you will install a single toner cartridge instead of separate ink cartridges. As always, follow the manual's instructions closely. Or, if it's written in the worst kind of Techno-Pidgin, put it to one side and trust to common sense.

The ins and outs

For the first time, we're going to bring together hardware and the three types of software discussed on page 15.

Hardware. Pretty obvious, really – we need to connect the printer to the system unit. Printers generally use either a parallel cable or, much more commonly now, a USB cable. The latter is the case here. Note that printer manufacturers often fail to include a cable in the box – an unpardonable omission, in our opinion, that may see you scurrying down to your computer superstore before you can go any further.

Windows. Depending upon the make, model and age of your printer, Windows may or may not recognise the printer automatically. In other words, it may just work and it may just not. Why?

Driver. It all hinges on whether Windows has a built-in copy of the necessary driver software. Remember, a driver helps a computer make sense of its hardware components. If Windows is lacking, no matter – you will find the driver you need on a CD-ROM supplied with the printer.

Program. Click the Print button in any program and whatever you see on screen – a letter, say, or a full-colour digital image – materialises on paper. It's as simple as that. A printer without any programs to keep it busy is a dull thing indeed. Moreover, many printers ship with extra programs that let you design greetings card and t-shirt transfers and so forth.

Unpacking and setting up

With lots of moving parts, printers are vulnerable to damage during transit. This is why they usually arrive trussed up like oven-ready turkeys. Your first task is to extract the device from its polystyrene shell, dig out the manual, and unpeel all the sticky tape. Next, attach any supplied paper input and output trays or feeders. Now pause and follow the instructions very carefully indeed. You might be told to plug the printer straight into the system unit, switch it on and see what happens; or you might have a couple of other preparatory steps to complete first.

In this example, the printer comes with a separate print head – a device that controls the flow of ink from the cartridges onto the page – that must be installed prior to use. However, some printer manufacturers use a different system whereby each ink cartridge incorporates its own print head. In this case, Step 2 will not apply.

With the computer turned off, connect the stubby square end of a USB cable to the port on the rear of the printer and the flat rectangular end to a USB port on the system unit. Connect the power cable to the mains electricity and turn the printer on.

After a few moments, the internal print head holder inside the printer moves to a central position. Open the front cover and raise the locking lever. Now carefully remove the print head from its packaging and, taking great care not to touch the nozzles or electrical contacts, slide the device into position.

Now lock the print head into position with the lever and install the ink cartridges. This printer has four: black, cyan, magenta and yellow. Again, follow the directions carefully and handle the ink with care. Close the cover when the cartridges are all in place. Finally, turn the printer off in preparation for the next procedure.

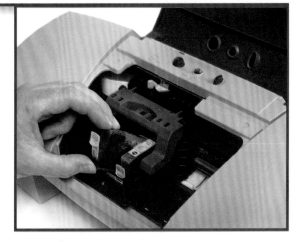

Installing the printer

Windows XP is pretty clever when it comes to printers, and if you've got a USB printer then installing it can be as simple as switching on your PC, plugging the USB cable into a spare USB port and waiting a few seconds for Windows to recognise it. However, modern printers are capable of lots of clever things and Windows doesn't necessarily know how to use the most useful features. That's why most printers come with a CD of software: the CD contains the necessary bits and bobs that enable you to get the most from your machine.

In most cases you should install the software before you connect the printer. That's certainly the case for the Brother printer we've used in this walkthrough, but in some cases your printer manufacturer needs you to connect the printer before you install anything. It doesn't make a difference to the actual software installation, but if you do things the wrong way round you might encounter problems – so it makes sense to get it right first time. You'll find details of the method the manufacturer wants you to use in the printed manual or, if your printer comes with one, the printed Quick Start guide.

Switch on your PC (if it isn't on already) and put the printer software CD into the CD drive. It should load automatically. If it doesn't, go into My Computer, look for the CD drive and double-click it; you should then see a file called Setup or Install. Double-click it to run the setup program. Whichever method you used, you should then see the introductory screen; in this case we need to choose the language we want to use (English).

Typically your CD will include lots of different programs – not just the printer software, but additional programs that might come in handy such as Adobe Reader, which you can use to read PDF document files. For now, though, we'll stick with the main printer software which, in the case of our Brother printer, is called MFL-Pro suite. Click the appropriate button to continue.

❸

One day computer firms will let us install their programs without wading through lots of legal jargon, but for now we're stuck with the legalese. It's worth checking to make sure there aren't any nasty clauses in the licence agreement (although such things are incredibly rare); when you've done that, or if you just want to press on, click Yes to accept the agreement. If you choose No, the installation program will exit.

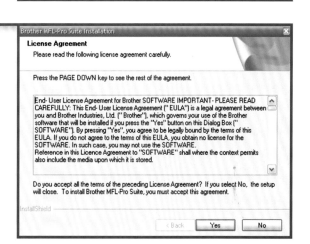

❹

Unfortunately, that's not the end of the legal stuff: if – like most printer CDs – you need to install several different programs, you'll have to accept or decline the licence agreement for each one. Once again, if you say No then the installation procedure will come to an abrupt end.

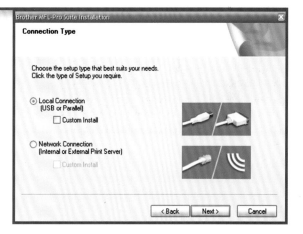

❺

Our Brother printer can be used in two ways: as a local printer, which means it's directly connected to our PC, or as a network printer, which means it can be shared among several machines on the same network. If we were using it on a network we'd need to connect it to the network router – essentially a box that connects PCs together – via an Ethernet cable, and the setup program would then install the necessary software to make the printer work on the network. However, in this case we're using it as a local printer, so we'll make sure the Local Connection box is checked and then press Next to continue.

❻

It's time to get connected. The USB cable should already be connected to your printer, so stick the other end into a spare USB port on your PC and switch the printer on. Click Next to continue and Windows will pop up a few messages to let you know that it's found your printer and that it's happily installing the necessary software.

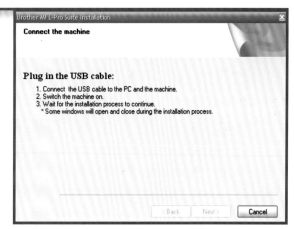

7

At the end of the installation process you'll usually be asked if you want to register. We can register in two ways: with Brother to activate the warranty, and with ScanSoft (the firm whose software is actually on the CD) to stay up to date with updates and special offers. To register, click the appropriate button and your web browser will take you to the registration page (assuming you have an active internet connection). Close your browser when you've finished and click Next to continue. If you don't want to register just now, click Next.

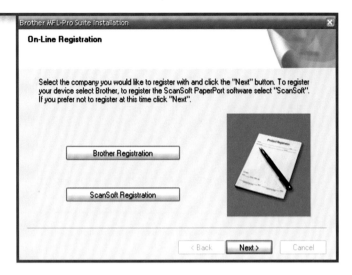

8

When Microsoft released Windows XP, they promised that the days of restarting your PC after installing new programs were long gone. They lied! Before you can start using your printer, you'll need to restart your computer. You can do this by clicking Finish now, or by manually restarting your PC from the Start menu later on.

9

Once your PC has been restarted, you're ready to go. When you install a Brother printer, it displays this Diagnostics screen to show that everything's OK. It's a once-only thing, so you don't need to worry about it annoying you every time you run Windows.

Tweaking the printer settings

Modern printers can do much more than simply rattle off printed text, although of course they can do that too. You can adjust the way in which they print photos, tell them the kind of paper they're using – it makes a difference; if you print on expensive photo paper but don't tell the printer you're using it, you won't get the best possible results – and even get them to manage the amount of ink they use. In this walkthrough we'll show you how to find and change these settings.

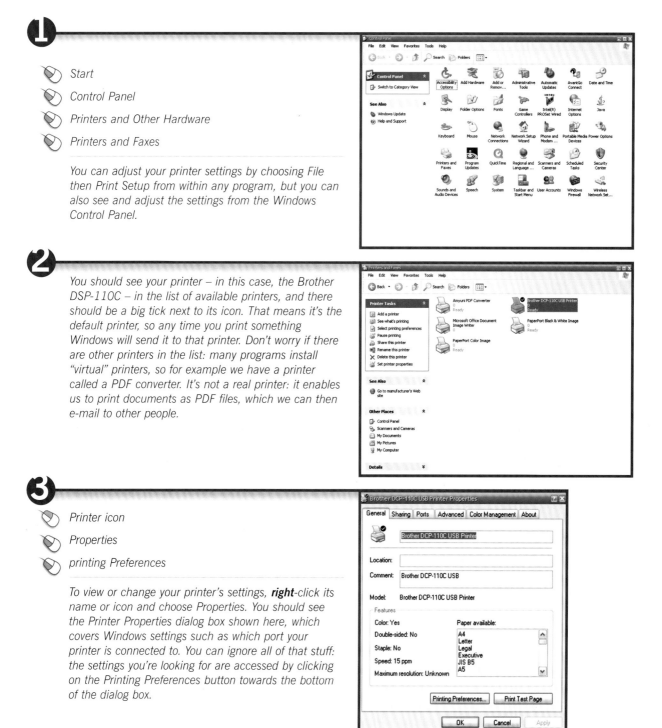

1

👆 *Start*

👆 *Control Panel*

👆 *Printers and Other Hardware*

👆 *Printers and Faxes*

You can adjust your printer settings by choosing File then Print Setup from within any program, but you can also see and adjust the settings from the Windows Control Panel.

2

You should see your printer – in this case, the Brother DSP-110C – in the list of available printers, and there should be a big tick next to its icon. That means it's the default printer, so any time you print something Windows will send it to that printer. Don't worry if there are other printers in the list: many programs install "virtual" printers, so for example we have a printer called a PDF converter. It's not a real printer: it enables us to print documents as PDF files, which we can then e-mail to other people.

3

👆 *Printer icon*

👆 *Properties*

👆 *printing Preferences*

*To view or change your printer's settings, **right**-click its name or icon and choose Properties. You should see the Printer Properties dialog box shown here, which covers Windows settings such as which port your printer is connected to. You can ignore all of that stuff: the settings you're looking for are accessed by clicking on the Printing Preferences button towards the bottom of the dialog box.*

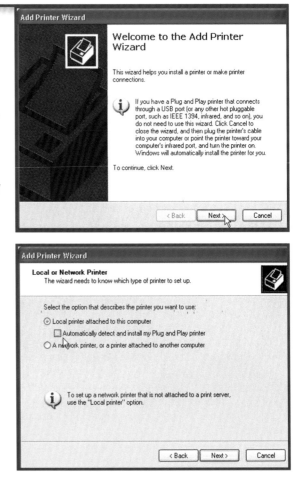

OK

The window that appears depends on the type of printer you have, but in most cases you can use the Printing Preferences dialog box to change the default page size, tell the printer what kind of paper you're using, and whether it should save ink (you'll find that setting under the Advanced tab). When you've made your changes, click OK to confirm them and then close the Printer Properties dialog box.

Parallel lines

If your printer doesn't have a USB port and/or you would rather use the parallel interface, the 'plug-and-play' routine described above may not work. In such cases, use the following method:

Start

Control Panel

Printers and Other Hardware icon

Add a printer

*This launches the Add Printer Wizard. Follow the step-by-step directions, being sure to specify that you're installing a local rather than a network printer (which would be connected to another computer). Also remove the tick next to 'Automatically detect and install my **Plug and Play** printer' box by clicking the box. This, incidentally, is an example of **'checking'** an option: one click adds a tick, or check mark; another click removes it.*

However, we must stress that it is far preferable to use a USB-capable printer and cable. Installation is easier and the printer itself will do its stuff faster.

PART 2 Connecting the scanner

Printers may be devilishly complex devices but scanners are comparatively simple. Essentially, a flatbed scanner – which looks like a small photocopier – takes a digital picture of whatever you place under the lid. This picture is then transferred to your computer, whereupon you can view and tweak it with an image-editing program. It needs no routine maintenance beyond an occasional wipe with a cloth, no refills, and should serve you well for years.

There are other types of scanners, notably handheld devices that you pass over a page, but flatbeds are the norm for home use.

Installation

Thanks to a universal driver standard called *TWAIN*, it is possible to 'import' an image from a scanner into all manner of programs. You might wish to scan a snapshot and enhance it on your computer by digitally removing flash-induced red-eye, for

A scanner takes digital pictures that can be imported into programs and saved as files on your computer's hard disk.

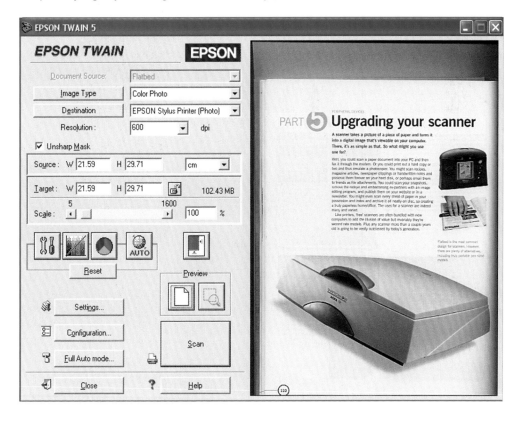

Don't forget to 'unlock' your scanner before attempting to use it!

example; or convert a newspaper article into editable text (a process known as Optical Character Recognition). Even word processors and spreadsheet programs can usually import images straight from a scanner.

Virtually all modern scanners now use the USB interface, which makes installation a breeze. However, the device will likely be protected by all manner of packaging and tape upon arrival. All this is easily removed, but there's one very important task that you _must_ perform. The scanning mechanism itself, which is located under the glass plate, is secured during transit. You must locate and unlock the release mechanism before you use your scanner. As always, check the manual for directions. Some releases, as in our example, are commendably obvious, but your device may have a tiny catch tucked away on the underside of the scanner's housing.

Installing the driver, which is of course essential to get your scanner working, is very straightforward. With your computer turned on and windows running, first connect the scanner to the system unit with a USB cable, and then turn it on. Windows will launch something called the Found New Hardware Wizard, which is essentially just a step-by-step installation routine. Ensure that the default 'Install the software automatically' option is checked – if not, click the little circle to check it – and pop the driver CD-ROM in its drive. Now click the Next button and follow the directions.

Let a Windows Wizard do the work.

Using your scanner

Now that you've installed your scanner, let's do something useful with it.

*Every scanner comes with its own scanning software, and while the programs do the same job they all do it in slightly different ways. For this walkthrough we'll use Google's free Picasa program (**www.picasa.google.com**). This is worth downloading even if you already have scanning software, as it's a great photo organiser too.*

Click Import and you'll be taken to the Import screen. The first thing we need to do is to tell Picasa where to get our scan from, so click the Select Device button and choose your scanner from the drop-down. In this example we're using a Brother USB printer/scanner.

No matter what scanner you use, you'll now see the scanning dialog. We're going to scan a colour photo, so make sure that the Color Picture button is checked. The next step is to do a quick preview scan to make sure everything's okay.

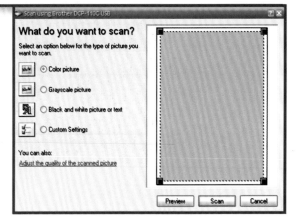

4

Click the Preview button and after a few seconds you'll see a rough scan of your picture or document. As you can see in this screenshot we're scanning a book upside down, but that's not a problem: we can fix that with a click later on.

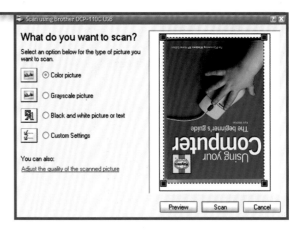

You'll often find that the scanner scans a wider area than just the photo or document you want to use. You can adjust the scanning area by dragging the points on each corner of the preview window. In this screenshot we've reduced the scanning area so we get our book cover but not the background.

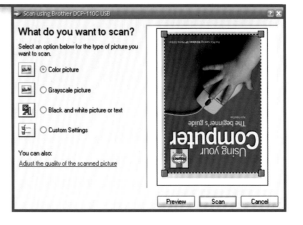

6

Click Scan and your scanner will start to scan the photo or document. You'll notice that it takes a bit longer than the preview scan. That's because this time the scanner is doing it properly. Picasa displays a progress bar in the bottom left of the screen to show you how much scanning is left to do.

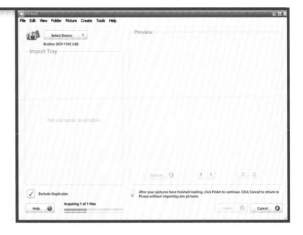

Once the scanning process is complete, you'll see a preview of the finished picture in the right-hand side of the window. If the scan isn't quite right – for example, because the photo is squint, or too dark – then click the Cancel button and start again.

8

As we mentioned earlier, scanning upside-down isn't a problem. If you look below and to the right of the preview image, you'll see two rotate buttons. The leftmost one rotates the image 90 degrees to the left; the rightmost, to the right. So to turn your image the right way up it's just a matter of clicking one of the rotate buttons twice.

9

When you click the Finish button, Picasa will create a new folder for your image, and it will ask you to give that folder a name. If you wish you can also add additional details to remind you when you did the scan, or why you were scanning it, or you can leave those sections blank. Click Finish to continue.

10

Picasa will now take you to the main program window, with your new scan in pride of place. You'll see that there's a toolbar at the bottom of the screen, but it's faded out: click your scan in the main window and the toolbar will come to life.

11

The toolbar enables you to carry out basic image tasks: giving your image a label, printing it out, e-mailing it or exporting it to another folder. You can also rotate your image, or use the slider at the top right of the toolbar to zoom in or out. However, if you double-click your image you'll get to see the fun stuff.

12

Double-clicking an image in Picasa keeps the toolbar at the bottom but opens a new one on the left-hand side of the screen. From this toolbar you can straighten wonky scans, get rid of redeye from photos, or adjust the brightness and contrast to make a scan clearer.

13

Picasa also enables you to add special effects: click the Effects tab and you'll see a range of options including Sharpen, Filtered B&W, Glow, Sepia and so on. To apply an effect just click it and the main image will update; in this screenshot we've used a sepia effect to make our image look as if it's very old.

14

If you wish, you can now export your image from Picasa for use in other programs. The Image Size options is particularly handy, because high-resolution scans can take up lots of disc space. If you're planning to e-mail a picture, it's a good idea to reduce the size of your picture with the 'Resize To' slider.

Moving on: turning scans into text

15

When you buy a scanner you'll often get an OCR program, which is short for Optical Character Recognition. This can turn your scans into editable text, and it's a real time-saver if like us, you often need to take paper documents and bring them up to date. In this walkthrough we'll use the PaperPort software that came free with our Brother scanner. Your software might look slightly different, but it'll work in the same way.

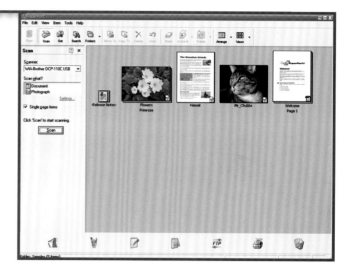

16

Before you can turn your scan into text, you need to give the program a scan to work with. Click Scan and as before, you'll get the Windows scanning dialog box. However this time we don't want to stick with the basic options: click Adjust The Quality of the Scanned Picture.

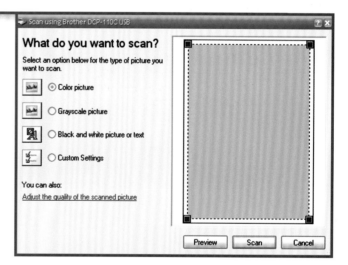

17

The Advanced Properties box will appear. For text documents it's a good idea to increase the resolution from the default 100 dots per inch to 300 dots per inch: this means the text in your scan will be crisp and clean, which makes the software's job an awful lot easier.

18

Once you've adjusted the scanning options you'll be returned to the scanning dialog box. As with other scans, click on Preview and adjust the scanning area so it doesn't include anything that might confuse the software, such as shadows. Click Scan to continue.

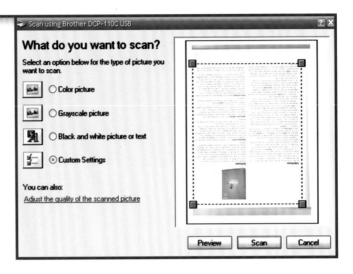

19

 Once the document has been scanned it will appear in the main window of your OCR program. It's a good idea to make some quick adjustments to improve the text recognition system's accuracy, so double-click your scan to open the editing window.

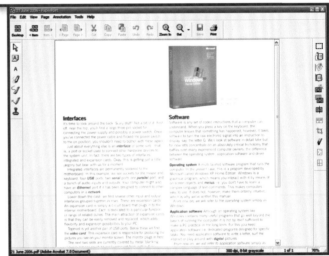

20

The toolbar at the right of the screen provides a number of adjustment options, including an Enhance button. Click it and the software will adjust the brightness and contrast to make the text darker and the background whiter. If you wish, you can make more adjustments – just say Yes when the software asks if you want to use the advanced options.

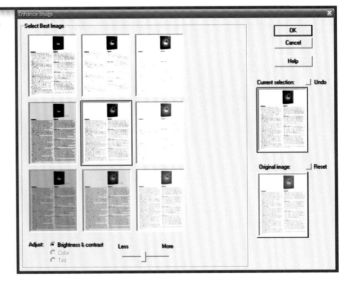

21

Once you've adjusted the brightness and contrast the result should look like this, with clear black text on a crisp white background. If your software includes a crop button –most programs do – it's a good idea to crop your document so only the text remains. Once you're happy with the image, click the Back to Desktop button to return to the main program window.

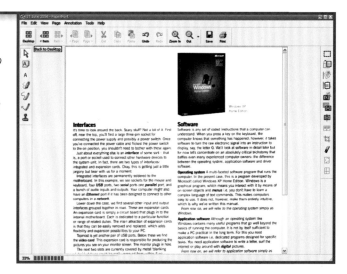

22

Now for the fun bit. The icons at the bottom of the PaperPort screen represent programs, so the third icon from the left – the notepad with a pencil – is WordPad, Windows' built-in word processor. To turn your scan into editable text, simply drag it from the main window and drop it over the WordPad icon.

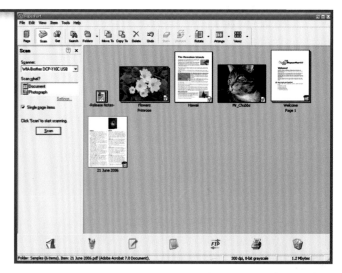

23

After a few seconds, WordPad will open with the editable text inside it. You might have to scroll down through some nonsense text before you get to the text you want. As you can see, PaperPort does a good job: all we need to do now is highlight the text we want and copy and paste it into another document.

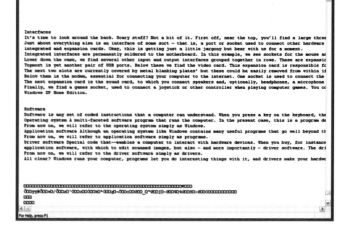

3

start

Windows XP

As we remarked earlier, Windows is a graphical, point-and-clicky, touchy-feely kind of operating system. The upshot is that once you've mastered a few simple concepts, your computer becomes remarkably easy to use (this wasn't always the case but the XP generation has helped matters enormously). Almost regardless of what you want to do, the same rules and steps apply.

Windows is always in a state of change, whether it's the latest patch, the addition of a new feature, the release of a major 'service pack' or the launch of an entirely new version like Windows Vista (scheduled for sale throughout 2007). However, Windows XP is here for some time to come and we believe that your first computer is likely to be running XP. The lessons you'll learn here can be easily transferred to Vista when you upgrade.

Key concepts

Windows typically provides ten ways to do anything and is loaded with smart shortcuts and time-saving tricks. But that way lies complexity and confusion. Here we stick to the most logical and straightforward, if not necessarily the quickest, methods of getting from A to B.

The Desktop

When you turn on your computer and Windows starts, your starting point is always the Desktop. The key areas are these:

Icons

Clickable links to programs and folders. In this example, there are five on view, but your computer's Desktop may look rather different depending on how your supplier has customised your system. Note that if you point at an icon without clicking, you'll get a pop-up bubble with a little information about it. This is called a screen tip.

My Documents *A folder on the hard disk used to store files that you create when you work with programs. You can also access all other folders from here. We'll work with My Documents in detail on page 83.*

My Computer *A quick way to find information about your computer's hardware, including its drives.*

My Network Places *Only relevant if your computer is linked to other computers or connected to the internet (as it will be in Part 4).*

Internet Explorer *A web browser. That is to say, the program that you'll use to view web pages on the internet.*

Recycle Bin *An important one. When you delete a file from your computer's hard disk, instead of disappearing irretrievably it actually gets stored in the Recycle Bin. This effectively gives you a chance to recover any file deleted by mistake – and believe us, you'll delete plenty of files by mistake as you work with your computer!*

Background *Just a picture to brighten up your day. In fact, it can be any picture you like.*

The Start Menu *See over the page for a detailed description of this important item.*

Taskbar A strip running across the bottom of the screen that shows you what's going on. At the far left, we find the Start button, which we'll consider in detail in a moment. At the far right is the Notification Area which shows which programs are working quietly in the *background*. The central part of the Taskbar is used to display buttons that relate to current activity.

QUICK Q & A

Q: The only icon I have on my Desktop is the Recycle Bin.

A: No problem. Look for My Documents, My Computer, My Network Places and Internet Explorer in the Start menu. right-click each one in turn and check the Show on Desktop option.

Desktop delights

Your Desktop is a very useful working space on which you can save files and folders and from which you can launch programs. Here's a run through of just some of the things you can do with it.

 Start button

All Programs

Accessories

Calculator

Send To

Desktop (create shortcut)

You normally launch computer programs through the Start menu but you can easily create a shortcut on the Desktop. Use this method to create a shortcut to the Windows Calculator. You can now double-click the new icon on your Desktop to launch the program without having to open the Start menu.

Desktop

Arrange Icons By

uncheck Auto Arrange

By default, Windows lines up Desktop icons in columns. However, if you uncheck the Auto Arrange feature, you can drag icons around the Desktop and place them anywhere you like. Try this now with your new Calculator shortcut. Just left-click the icon, hold down the mouse key, and drag the icon to a new spot on the Desktop. Release the mouse key and the icon will stay put. Check Auto Arrange at any time to reorder your icons.

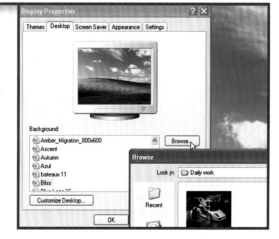

Desktop

Properties

Desktop tab

Not happy with the Desktop background, or 'wallpaper'? You can change it here. Select a new picture from the built-in menu and click Apply then OK. Alternatively, use the Browse button to find one of your own pictures. You might want to do this when you've transferred some of your snapshots from a digital camera.

④

 Windows key + D

This handy keyboard shortcut takes you straight to the Desktop at any time. Imagine you have six open windows and you want to find a file that's stored on your Desktop or launch a program via a Desktop shortcut (or perhaps your boss walks in while you're in the middle of playing a computer game). Just press the Windows key and the D key simultaneously and all windows will be instantly minimised, leaving just the Desktop visible. To return to where you were, repeat this keyboard shortcut and all windows will reopen.

Taskbar tricks

The taskbar remains visible on screen even when the Desktop is completely covered in windows. Its most obvious and useful function is to allow you to switch between windows and between programs. Let's see this in action.

①

 My Computer icon

This opens a window with information about your computer. Note that an important change has occurred on the Taskbar. A button called My Computer has appeared. Try clicking this button once. The My Computer window disappears from your screen and you're back to the plain Desktop again. All that's happened here is that My Computer has been 'minimised' to the Taskbar i.e. the window is still open but temporarily reduced to a button. Click the button again and up pops the My Computer window.
    Minimise My Computer once more.

②

Recycle Bin icon

Open the Recycle Bin by double-clicking its Desktop icon. Now there are two buttons on the Taskbar. Practise clicking these buttons to manipulate the windows. For instance, you can keep both windows minimised at the same time, or have one open on the Desktop with the other minimised, or have both windows open on the Desktop simultaneously. The button corresponding to whichever window is currently open looks as if it has been depressed on the Taskbar. If you have both windows open, the button corresponding to the 'active' window is depressed. Active simply means the window you're currently working with or opened most recently.

3

🖱️ *Taskbar*

To automatically organise open windows on the Desktop, right click a clear area on the Taskbar – i.e. avoid the buttons – and select one of the menu options. You have your windows arranged in several ways so just experiment. For instance, the Cascade option arranges them one on top of the other.

4

🖱️ *Taskbar*

🖱️ *Toolbars*

🖱️ *Quick Launch*

Again, right-click a clear spot on the Taskbar and put a tick against the Quick Launch toolbar. You'll find that three new buttons appear just next to the Start menu. Usually, these will be Internet Explorer (your web browser), Outlook Express (your e-mail program) and Show Desktop. These are handy for launching the programs you'll probably use most. Show Desktop simply mimics the keyboard shortcut we showed you in the previous section.

5

🖱️ *Taskbar*

🖱️ *Properties*

🖱️ *Group similar taskbar buttons*

By default, Windows will group buttons together on the Taskbar. Say you have three web pages open: you'll find only one Taskbar button for all three, with a fiddly pop-up menu for selecting between them. We and everybody we know find this intensely irritating, hence this recommendation: turn off the grouping feature! Now you'll get a new button on the Taskbar for every open window, web page and program.

6

The disadvantage with the above step is that when you're busy multitasking, your Taskbar can eventually run out of room for new buttons. No problem: just point at the top edge of the Taskbar, wait until the mouse cursor changes to a double-headed arrow, then drag the Taskbar up the screen until it doubles in height. Now there's plenty of room for buttons. Reverse the drag operation to restore the Taskbar to its original height.

My Network
Places

The Start Menu

You could sit and stare at the Desktop all day, but to do something useful you need the Start button and its corresponding menu. Click it once and you'll see something like this. What can it all mean?

Owner

Current User *Here you see your name and a picture of your choosing. Or, rather, you don't but will on page 163.*

Pinned Programs *This section contains fixed links to certain programs. Internet Explorer (a web browser) and Outlook Express (an e-mail program) are always 'pinned' here but you can add other programs, too.*

Internet
Internet Explorer

E-mail
Outlook Express

Frequently Used Programs *This section updates all the time to reflect the six programs you use most, aside from any that appear in the pinned programs section.*

Paint Shop Pro 6
6

Tour Windows XP

Windows Media Player

Windows Movie Maker

WordPad

Windows Messenger

All Programs *Click here to access a full list of all the software installed on your computer. We were here earlier in the mouse and keyboard sections when we launched Solitaire and WordPad. A right-pointing arrow next to a menu entry indicates that the entry can be expanded. Some of these 'sub-menus' can themselves be further expanded (see above). Note that to save time you merely have to point at an entry on the Start Menu to make it expand; only click an entry when you want to launch the program.*

As you install more and more software on your computer, you'll begin to see the attraction of the Pinned Programs and Frequently Used Programs sections of the Start Menu. They provide useful shortcuts to the programs that you use most often and save you always having to root through the All Programs list.

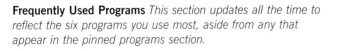

All Programs

start

My Documents

My Pictures

My Music

My Computer

Control Panel

Help and Support

Search

Run...

QUICK Q & A

What are those funny balloons that keep popping up from the Taskbar?
That's just Windows trying to tell you something. Don't be shy – click on the balloon to find out more. One very important balloon may prompt you to 'activate' your copy of Windows XP (if your supplier hasn't already done this on your behalf). You can do this over the internet or by telephone. Just follow the Wizard's directions.

Shortcuts *The upper section on the right side of the Start Menu contains links to frequently used storage folders and hardware information. These effectively duplicate the functions of the My Documents and My Computer icons on the Desktop.*

Control Panel *A link to the Control Panel wherein you tweak your computer's hardware settings (as, in fact, we did earlier when we slowed down the mouse and keyboard).*

Help and Support *This is a link to Windows' own help centre, an area that we'd encourage you to frequent regularly.*

Search *Lost a file somewhere on your hard disk? The Search tool can help you find it see page 87.*

Run *A way of launching and installing programs with typed text commands. Not, it has to be said, a favourite activity of ours.*

Log Off/Turn Off Computer *The second option you've already used and will continue to use every time you want to turn off your computer. The Log Off option, however, provides a way of leaving Windows in order to let somebody else start a new Windows session on the same computer. Sounds confusing? Not at all. Skip to Appendix 3 for details.*

So, in short, the Start button fires up the Start Menu, and this gets you started. To close the menu, simply click the Start button again, or press the Escape key, or click any blank spot on the Desktop or the Taskbar, or ... (see, we told you that there are 10 ways to do anything in Windows).

Log Off   Turn Off Computer

Getting comfortable with windows

Whenever you open a program or perform a task on your computer, the action takes place inside a self-contained box on your monitor screen, called a window. Each open window is (more or less) independent of all others and, as we have seen, you can switch between windows using the Taskbar. Here we look at a typical window's key features.

My Computer

QUICK Q & A

Q: How do I see more/less on my monitor screen?
A: This is down to screen resolution. The lower the resolution, the bigger everything appears but the less room you have for lots of windows; increase the resolution and windows and icons shrink, but you can squeeze more onto the screen at any one time. Consult your monitor's manual to check which resolutions it 'supports' (i.e. can work with), and experiment here:

- Start
- Control Panel
- Appearance and Themes icon
- Change the screen resolution
- [move screen resolution slider]
- Apply

Title Bar. *The shaded top edge of a window displays the name of the program or process in question. The Title Bar also has three important little buttons.*

The first button minimises the window (i.e. turns it into a button on the Taskbar). To restore it, you click the Taskbar button.

The middle button maximises the window so that it takes up all available screen space. Click it again to restore the window to its original size.

The final button should be familiar by now: it closes the window.

You can also click any point on the title bar, hold down the mouse button, drag the window to a different position on the screen and then drop it in place (as we saw back on page 32). Don't forget that you can resize windows, too (see page 32).

Menu bar *A number of clickable menus containing organised control and configuration options. The contents of each menu depends upon the program or process. WordPad, for instance, has a rather different set of menus.*

Toolbar *Clickable buttons. Again, these relate to the program or the process and vary considerably.*

Scrollbar *When it's not possible to see the entire contents of a window all at one time, a scrollbar appears. This lets you scroll up and down and through the window. Either click-and-drag the scrollbar slider or click the little arrows above and below the scrollbar (or to the left and right in the case of a horizontal scrollbar).*

Pane *Windows may be sub-divided into separate sections. Each section is, predictably enough, called a window pane.*

In Windows, you can only do something (perform a task, click an icon, type some text, whatever) within one window, the 'active' window, at any one time. You can tell which window is currently active in two ways: a depressed Taskbar button, and an emboldened title bar. In the screenshot below for instance, the My Computer window is clearly active. To make the Recycle Bin active, you would click its Taskbar button.

When you have two or more windows open, you can use the Taskbar to automatically arrange them on screen, as we discussed a couple of pages ago. You can also close windows and programs directly from the Taskbar. Right-click a button and left-click Close from the pop-up menu. If the program requires your attention before it can be closed – for example, you may have work that should be saved before closing a program – you will be prompted to take the required action.

Tiling your windows is one way of keeping several open on screen at the same time. Remember, though, that you can only work with the active window at any given time.

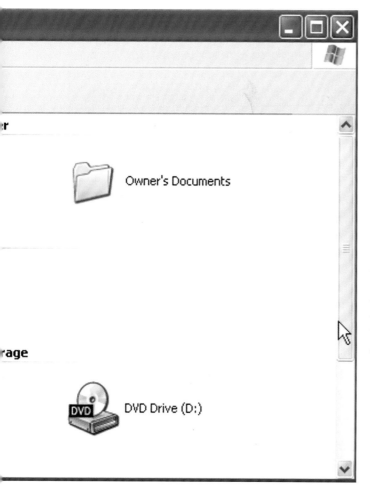

Owner's Documents

rage

DVD Drive (D:)

The Windows Control Panel

The Windows Control Panel is a wonderful thing: with it you can change almost everything Windows does, from the way it looks to the way it performs. In this section we'll discover the key Control Panel components that can make your system sing.

To go to the Control Panel, click the Start Menu and choose Control Panel from the list at the right. You should now see a screen like this one; if the version on your computer has a lot more options and a white background instead of a blue one, click Switch To Category View at the top-left of the window.

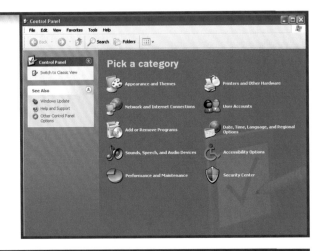

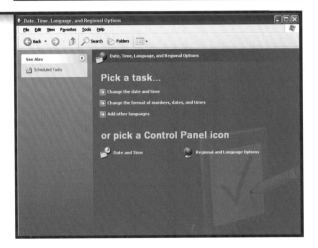

As you'd expect, if you click Appearance and Themes you can change the way Windows looks. There are four options: you can change the computer's theme, so for example you can change from a blue colour scheme to a silver or green one; you can change the picture that appears as your desktop background; you can change the screen saver; and you can change the screen resolution.

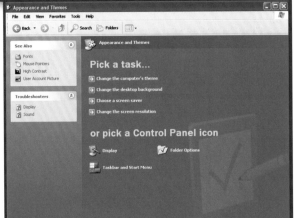

If you want to adjust Windows' clock, change the way in which Windows displays numbers and dates or install a new language, you can do it from Control Panel's Date, Time, Language and Regional Options section.

4

Sounds, Speech and Audio Devices is where you can adjust your speaker set-up – Windows can work with standard stereo speakers or multi-channel surround sound systems, and you can tell it which kind you're using for the best results. If you click Advanced Volume Controls you can even adjust the volume for different things, such as the CD player or a microphone (if you have one).

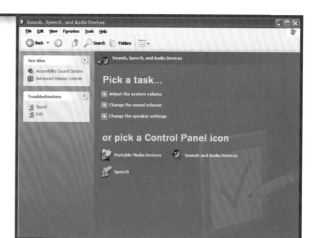

5

The Network and Internet Connections section enables you to add a new internet connection, create a home office network or connect to a wireless network. You can also use it to adjust your current internet settings. To do this, double-click Internet Options.

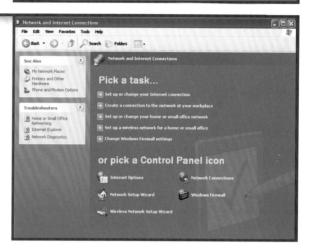

6

As you can see, the Internet Properties window that appears is organised into different tabs. In the General tab, you can change your home page – the first page that loads when you open Internet Explorer – or delete your internet browsing history. You can also change the list of search engines that appears in Internet Explorer's search bar (if you're using the latest version, Internet Explorer 7).

7

Click the Privacy tab to see how suspicious Internet Explorer should be. In this screenshot we're using Medium privacy, and you can fine-tune the settings by clicking on the Advanced button. If you're using Internet Explorer 7, you can also prevent sites from blasting you with pop-up adverts.

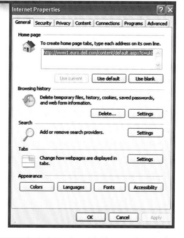

The Content tab is handy for parents: you can configure Internet Explorer so that it won't view sites that haven't been rated as family-friendly by the Internet Content Rating Association. Most big-name sites have been rated, although you'll find that more obscure sites haven't – so if you enable ratings you might not be able to access them.

Control Panel's Accessibility Options section is a boon for people with disabilities: you can make the display more suitable for partially sighted people, replace audio warnings with on-screen ones, and use keyboard shortcuts if you have difficulty using the mouse.

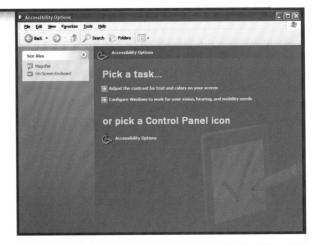

It's a good idea to make regular visits to the Performance and Maintenance section, which you can use to tweak Windows' settings in order to squeeze as much speed as possible from your system. To see the available options, click See Basic Information About Your Computer.

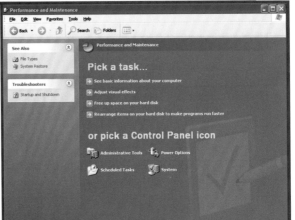

You should now see the System Properties dialog box shown here. If you want to improve your PC's performance, click the Advanced tab and look for the section headed Performance. Now click the Settings button.

12

Another dialog box should appear: this time, the Performance Options dialog shown here. Rather than using the 'best appearance' and 'best performance' options, it's a good idea to try disabling individual items such as 'Fade or Slide menus into view'. Such things look good, but they can make Windows feel slow sometimes.

13

Close the Performance Options dialog box and you'll be returned to the System Properties dialog box. Click Automatic Updates and you'll see a range of options that tell Windows how often it should check for updates and important patches for Windows. We'd recommend the Automatic option, which checks every time you're online and automatically downloads any critical updates for your system.

14

Close the System Properties dialog and you'll return to Control Panel's Performance and Maintenance screen. Click the 'Rearrange items...' option to open the Defragmenter. This is a utility that moves the files on your hard disk closer together, which can make your system run faster – but beware, because on a typical PC hard disk the process can take an hour or more, and the more stuff that's on your hard disk, the longer the process will take. It's a good idea to run Defragmenter when your PC's idle and you've got something else to do while it gets on with the job.

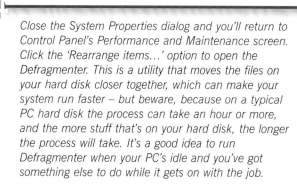

Why 'defragging' can speed up your PC

When Windows saves a file, it breaks it into bits and stores those bits in different places. This is a good thing, because it's designed to make the best use of the available storage. However, these days even the humblest PC has a massive hard disk, and the more widely spread a file becomes, the more time it takes to find the various pieces of a file when Windows needs it. Individually, the delay is tiny, but if you have thousands of files on your PC – which you do, because Windows alone consists of thousands of individual files – then as your files become more widely spread the delays add up to cause a noticeable drop in performance.

The answer is defragmentation, or 'defragging' as it's often called. When you defrag your hard disk, the individual bits of files scattered around your hard disk are brought closer together – which means Windows has to spend less time looking for them, and your system speeds up as a result. You don't need to defragment very often, but if you think your PC is getting a bit sluggish then defragging your hard disk could solve the problem.

PART 5 Files and folders

Sooner or later, you're going to create something on your computer that you want to save. You have a choice of storage locations, as we'll see in the very next section, but first it helps to get a handle on the notion of files and folders – and, specifically, how Windows XP works with them.

Here we see a hierarchy of folders in the left window pane with files within a selected folder displayed in the right pane. Your computer has many, many levels of files within folders within folders within folders . . .

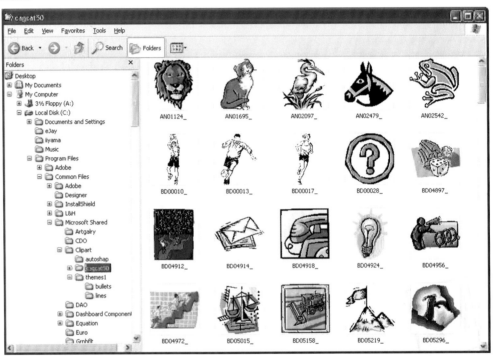

So what's a file?

A file is any single self-contained chunk of information stored in a digital format. A letter written on a word processor and saved to the hard disk is a file; an image created on or copied from a scanner or a digital camera is a file; a computer-generated sound recording is a file; a digital video clip is a file; even a computer program is a file (or, rather, a collection of files).

Although all files are essentially just a collection of 1s and 0s – that is, **binary data** – your computer has to be able to tell one file from another. Thus every file has two parts: a file name, and a file extension that tells the computer something about its format. When you make your own files, you choose the name as you go along, and you can be as creative or pedantic as you like. The extension, however, ties the file to a particular program or type of program, and needs to be chosen with care (when indeed there is a choice at all). An extension is usually 2, 3 or 4 letters long and tacked on to the file name proper with a dot separating them.

For example, let's say you write a letter in Word, the popular word processing program, and call it 'Hi Mum'. Word's default file extension is '.doc', so this file's full title becomes 'Hi Mum.doc'. Now, any other computer with a recent version of Word installed can open, read and edit this file. You will, of

course, be able to open it yourself whenever you like.

Some file formats and their associated extensions are proprietary. The '.doc' format belongs to Microsoft, for instance, which effectively means that only Word and other Microsoft programs can create or open '.doc' files. (Actually, some other word processors can work with '.doc' files but only by means of special import filters.)

However, many file formats are non-proprietary, which means that they are compatible with a wider range of programs. A sound recording, for instance, might be saved in the common .wav format and opened with just about any program capable of playing sound files. A web page – which is, after all, just another file – will generally have an .htm or .html extension, and any web browser the world over can view it.

The only time you really have to worry about file formats and extensions is when you want to share your files. That is, if you write a report in Word and save it with the '.doc' file extension, you should first ensure that all intended recipients of the file have a copy of Word on their computers. Failing that, you can choose an alternative non-proprietary file extension. In the case of text files, this would generally be '.txt' or '.rtf'.

OK, so what's a folder?

A folder is a file holder. Just as you might keep your paper documents in a series of folders in a filing cabinet, so on a computer you save files in the virtual equivalent of folders. A folder is just an organisational tool – a gimmick, if you like – designed to make file management intuitive and sensible.

Moreover, Windows lets you work with a hierarchy of 'nested' files and folders (i.e. files within folders within folders within folders, and so on, more or less forever). The advantage is that you can organise your work in such a way that it's easy to retrieve any individual file in moments. When you consider that your computer's hard disk can easily hold *millions* of files, good file management is truly essential.

Say you write a letter to your bank manager on your computer, print out a hard copy and post it. You're going to want to keep a copy on your computer, and that means saving the letter as a file. But where, exactly? Let's imagine that you already have a folder called Home Finances. This sounds like a good starting point. However, you also keep details of household bills and standing orders and hire purchase agreements in here. What you need is a sub-folder within Home Finances called something like Bank Correspondence. Now *that* would be a good place to store your letter. Even if you completely forget where you've saved it, you should be able to track it down months or even years down the line.

But where do all these folders come from? The answer is that you make them yourself as you go along. It's time for some practical exercises.

Making folders

Here we will create a brand new folder on your computer's hard disk.

My Documents icon

Windows provides a very useful 'top-level' folder called My Documents. You'll find its icon on the Desktop. Double-click this icon to open the folder and inside you'll find two or three sub-folders: My Music, My Pictures and, perhaps, My Videos. These are simply the recommended locations for saving music, image and video files respectively. What you will not find is a Home Finances folder. So let's make one.

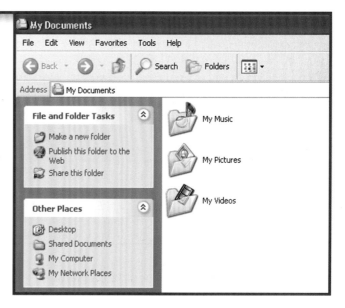

2

Make a new folder

This option is found in the left window pane in an area called File and Folder Tasks. If by chance your My Documents folder looks rather different from our screenshot and the File and Folder Tasks area is not visible, click the Folders button on the Toolbar (we'll be covering the different ways to view and work with folders later).

3

Home Finances [Enter]

*A new folder appears in the right-hand side of the My Documents window. It's given title is, boringly, New Folder, but we can change that. Because the words 'New Folder' are automatically highlighted at the point of creating the folder, all you have to do is **overtype** a new title. In this case, we're calling it Home Finances.*

4

New Folder icon

Rename this folder

Home Finances [Enter]

This step only applies if Step 3 goes wrong and you didn't manage to rename the folder while 'New Folder' was highlighted. Select New Folder by clicking its icon once. Now look in the left window pane and you'll see an option to Rename this folder. Click this and once again the folder's title becomes highlighted. Now just type in the new name and press the Enter key. Any folder can be renamed in this manner.

5

Home Finances icon

Make a new folder

Bank Correspondence [Enter]

Following the example discussed above, we now want to create a sub-folder within Home Finances called Bank Correspondence. Double-click the Home Finances folder icon to open the folder (which is, of course, currently empty). Now create and name a new folder just as in Steps 2 and 3 above. Once again, you can easily rename the folder as in Step 4 if anything goes wrong.

Saving and opening files

You now have a suitable home for a letter to your bank manager. Its file path (a rather ungainly method of specifying the location of any file or folder) is this:

My Documents\Home Finances\Bank Correspondence

Each slash (\) indicates that the following folder is a sub-folder of the previous folder. What you do not yet have is the letter itself, so let's create and save just such a file now.

1

- *Start*
- *All Programs*
- *Accessories*
- *WordPad*

Yes, it's back to trusty WordPad again. There's every chance that your computer system came with a fully-fledged word processor like Microsoft Word but this will do for now. Open the program and type a letter to your bank manager. Or rather, to save time, type anything you like, even just a word or two.

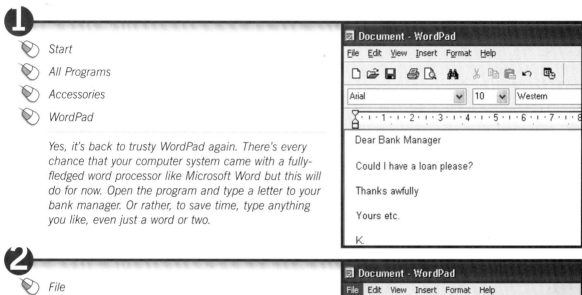

2

- *File*
- *Save As*

In some ways, this is the most important lesson in the entire manual. What you're about to do is save a file. Once saved, this file – any file – will be stored safely on your computer's hard disk. But until it is saved, the file doesn't really exist. A sudden power cut would obliterate it.
You'll find the File menu button on the far left of the Menu Bar. Click it once and down drops a drop-down menu. Move the mouse pointer down through the menu until Save As is highlighted, and then click once.

3

- *Home Finances icon*
- *Open*

The Save As window is where you pick a location for your file. As it happens, Windows expects you to save files in the My Documents folder or a folder within it, hence My Documents appears in the Save in: box automatically. Below this, you can see all the folders located within My Documents – and right there is your Home Finances folder. Click its icon to select it and then click the Open button.

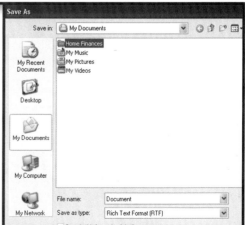

④

🖱️ *Bank Correspondence icon*

🖱️ *Open*

Now the Home Finances folder appears in the Save in: box and below it you can see the Bank Correspondence sub-folder. Select this now and click Open.

⑤

🖱️ *File name box*

⌨️ *Letter to bank manager requesting a loan*

You have navigated successfully to the Bank Correspondence folder, which is where your file will now be saved. In the File name: box near the bottom of the window, the word 'Document' appears. This is WordPad's default suggestion for file names but it would be a spectacularly uninspiring choice here. So, click once in the File name box to select 'Document' and replace it with your own file name. Click the Save button when you're through.

⑥

⌨️ *[edit file]*

⌨️ *[X]*

The Save As window disappears and you're back with your document again. Check the window's Title Bar and you'll see that it displays your chosen file name – proof that your file saving has been successful. You could print the file at this point (click the Print icon on the Toolbar), or close it (click the cross in the top-right corner of the window). However, try this first. Make some small change to the letter, such as adding or deleting a word or two. We replaced 'Thanks awfully' with 'Thanks very much'. Now try to close the window.

☰ Letter to bank manager requesting a loan - Word

File   Edit   View   Insert   Format   Help

Arial ⌄   10 ⌄   Western

Dear Bank Manager

Could I have a loan please?

Thanks awfully

Yours etc.

⑦

🖱️ *No*

WordPad identifies that the file you are currently trying to close is not the same in every respect as the file you originally saved with this file. This means that the original file is about to be overwritten by (that is, deleted and replaced with) this amended version, and so the program asks you whether this is indeed what you intend. It's a crucial point: if you click No, the changes you just made will be lost and the file will revert to its original form; click Yes and the file will be saved exactly as is and the original file will be lost forever. In this case, click No. See page 89 for more on saving and overwriting files.

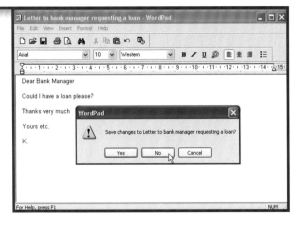

- ![mouse] *Start*
- ![mouse] *All Programs*
- ![mouse] *Accessories*
- ![mouse] *WordPad*
- ![mouse] *File*
- ![mouse] *Open*

Let's now suppose that you wish to find and read this file at some later date. We'll show you two ways to go about this. First, launch WordPad and click Open from the File menu.

- ![mouse] *Home Finances icon*
- ![mouse] *Open*
- ![mouse] *Bank Correspondence icon*
- ![mouse] *Open*
- ![mouse] *Letter to bank manager requesting a loan icon*
- ![mouse] *Open*

Now it's a case of navigating through folders until you find the letter. When you see your target file, select it and click Open once more.

- ![mouse] *My Documents icon*
- ![mouse] *Home Finances icon*
- ![mouse] *Bank Correspondence icon*

Alternatively, you can locate and open this (or any) file through the My Documents folder. Double-click the My Documents icon on the Desktop to open the folder in a window, and then double-click the Home Finances icon within it. Repeat with Bank Correspondence. Again, this is simply navigating through folders.

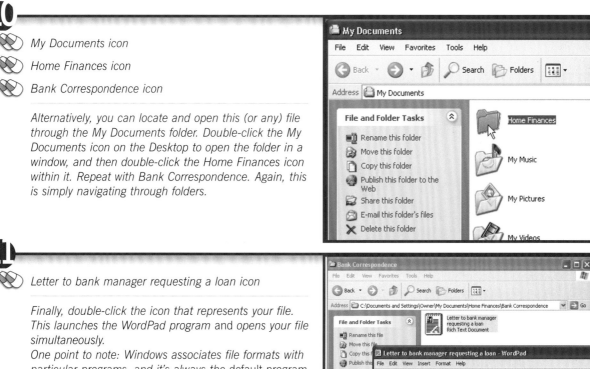

- ![mouse] *Letter to bank manager requesting a loan icon*

Finally, double-click the icon that represents your file. This launches the WordPad program and opens your file simultaneously.

One point to note: Windows associates file formats with particular programs, and it's always the default program that launches when you double-click a file. In this case, WordPad happens to be the default program for .rtf files – but if there was a second program capable of handling text files installed on this computer, like Word, it's possible that it would be associated with .rtf files instead. In other words, opening a file does not necessarily launch the program it was created in.

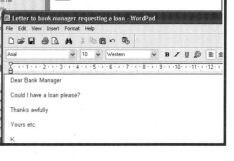

Deleting, recovering and searching for files. Oh, and a shortcut too

Windows offers two ways to manipulate files and folders: Task view and Folders view. The former, a new approach only introduced with Windows XP, is designed to make it easier and faster to perform common tasks. But is it? Let's find out.

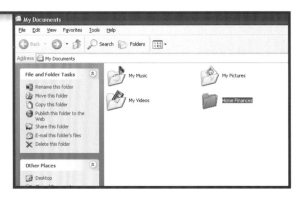

My Documents icon

Home Finances icon

The left pane of this window has links to things that Windows thinks you might want to do. These include renaming or moving a folder or file, copying it, sharing it with other people who use this computer, or e-mailing a folder's contents to a contact. You can also delete files and folders here. We'll do that now.

Delete this folder

Yes

With Home Finances folder selected in the window, click Delete this folder in the left pane. Up pops a box asking for final confirmation. Click Yes. And that's it – your Home Finances folder and all its contents has gone for good.

Recycle Bin icon

Home Finances icon

Restore this item

Actually, not quite. Remember what we said about the Recycle Bin earlier (p.68)? Double-click its Desktop icon now and inside you will find the deleted folder. Select this folder with a click and then click Restore this item in the left pane. As if by magic, the folder now reappears in your My Documents folder. It has been un-deleted.

④

Folders

Back at the My Documents window, click the Folders button on the Toolbar. The left pane changes to show the hierarchical structure of your computer's folders. This is more how Windows used to look. To expand any folder, click the '+' sign to the left of its icon. Although this is ideal for in-depth navigation, the chances are that pretty soon you'll lose track of where you are. This is why we heartily recommend sticking to the Task view!. Still, try to locate your letter file while you're here. Then click the Folders button once again to return to Task view.

⑤

Start

Search

Documents

Let's suppose that you haven't been terribly rigorous with your file management and have somehow misplaced your letter. Windows has a built-in search facility which you can access from the Start Menu. To speed things up, it helps if you specify what type of file you are looking for. In this case, it's a document. However, if you're not sure, just click the 'All files and folders' option. Ignore the daft dog.

⑥

 [keywords]

Search

You are now invited to enter any information that might narrow the search further. We'll use two keywords: letter and bank. You can also tell the dog, sorry, Windows when you last modified (worked with) the file. Click the Search button.

Letter to bank manager requesting a loan icon

Hey presto, there it is. Double-click the icon to open the file in Word Pad and immediately save it afresh in a sensible location that you won't forget (i.e. in a folder called Bank Correspondence within a folder called Home Finances within the My Documents folder).

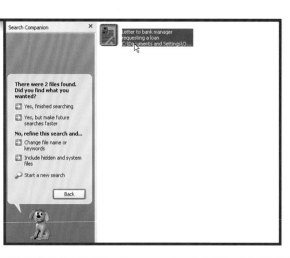

Letter to bank manager requesting a loan icon

Finally, one time-saving tip we just can't resist. When you work with particular folders or files frequently, you can place a shortcut to them right on the Desktop. This saves you having to navigate through the My Documents folder every time. Open the My Documents folder as before, find your letter, right-click the icon and hold down the mouse button. Now, still holding that right mouse button down, drag the icon out of the My Documents window and onto a clear space on the Desktop.

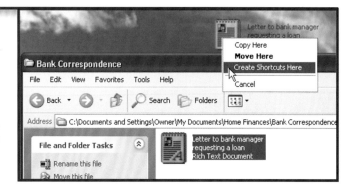

Create Shortcuts Here

Release the right mouse button and up pops a menu. Point at Create Shortcuts Here to select it and click once (back to the left mouse button now). The original file stays put in the Bank Correspondence folder but now there's a new icon on the Desktop. This, we stress, is not the file itself but merely a shortcut, or link, to the original file. You can now open the file at any time by double-clicking its shortcut.

Shortcut

Delete

Yes

You can delete a shortcut at any time without deleting or in any way affecting the original file. You know when an icon is a shortcut because it has an arrow in the bottom-left corner. This one is a shortcut to a folder

Different views

1

Using My Documents, you can also view your files and folders in several different ways: just select from the options in the View menu on the Menu Bar. Feel free to experiment. Filmstrip view is perfect for previewing pictures (available only in the special My Pictures folder).

2

Thumbnails gives you a small representation of the file.

3

Icons is ideal for dragging-and-dropping files. Tile view basically means bigger icons.

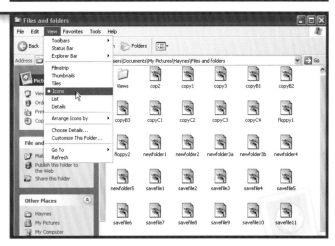

5

Use List or Details view when you need fuller information about your files.

Copying files and folders

You will sometimes want to move a file or a whole folder from one location on the hard disk to another. This is very easily accomplished in Windows in a number of ways. We'll break our keep-it-simple rule temporarily to look at three different methods, but only to give you the chance to find the best one for you.

1

- *My Documents icon*
- *Home Finances icon*
- *Bank Correspondence icon*
- *Letter to bank manager requesting a loan icon*
- *Copy this file*

Here we see the letter file once again. A single click on its icon selects the file. Now click Copy this file in the File and Folder Tasks pane on the left side of the window.

2

- *(+) My Documents*
- *My Music icon*
- *Copy*

When the Copy Items window appears, click the tiny '+' sign next to My Documents to expand the folder (i.e. show all its sub-folders). Then click on the My Music folder, and click the Copy button. This immediately saves a copy of your letter in the My Music folder while leaving the original file safely stored in the Bank Correspondence folder.

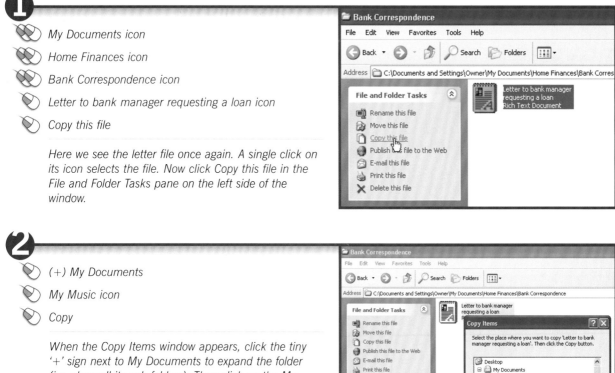

3

- *My Documents icon*
- *My Music icon*

But just to be sure, have a look in the My Music folder. There it is. Let's leave it there for time being and look at an alternative file management method.

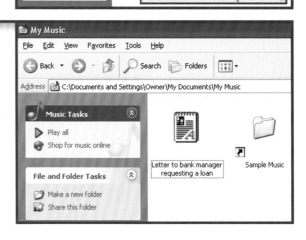

One of the reasons why we encouraged you to play Solitaire early on was to practise your drag-and-drop skills. Remember how you dragged playing cards from one column and dropped them on another? Well, you can also drag-and-drop files and folders, both within a single window or between windows. We'll look at these in turn.

1

Folders

(+) Home Finances

Starting precisely where you left off in the previous exercise – that is, with the My Music folder open – click the Folders button on the Toolbar. This replaces the Tasks pane on the left side of the window with a hierarchical Folders view of your computer. Now very carefully click the little + sign next to Home Finances. (If you accidentally click the Home Finances icon instead, just click the Back button on the Toolbar and try again.) The Bank Correspondence folder should now be visible in the Folders section of the left window pane.

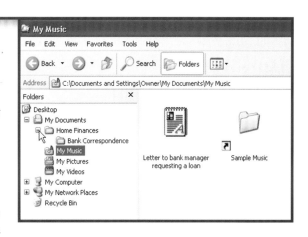

2

Sample Music icon

Now right-click the Sample Music icon and hold down the mouse button. Drag the Sample Music icon across the window and into the left-hand Folders view pane, and point at the Bank Correspondence folder. When Bank Correspondence becomes highlighted, release the right mouse button. (If you struggle with this, release the right mouse button at any time and abort the manoeuvre by clicking Cancel on the pop-up menu.)

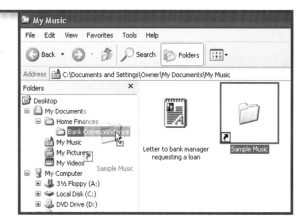

3

Copy Here

A pop-up menu now appears. Point at Copy Here and click once (back to the left button again). The Sample Music folder and all its contents is now copied to the Bank Correspondence folder. Feel free to check. Note that you can perform exactly the same move with individual files instead of folders.

Working with the Folder view can be fiddly so here's an alternative way to drag-and-drop files and folders. Try it and see – and, if it doesn't suit, just reverse the change you make in Step 1.

1

My Documents icon

Tools

Folder Options

Open each folder in its own window

Apply   OK

Until now we have been opening folders within a single My Documents window. Making this simple change has an interesting result that we'll see in the next step. Click the circle next to Open each folder in its own window to check that option, and then click Apply and OK.

2

My Music icon

Now double-click the My Music icon in the My Documents folder. As you can see, the folder opens in a brand new window. If necessary, click-and-drag the My Music window into a new position until you can see both its contents and My Documents at the same time (skip back to page 32 for help with moving windows). Our goal here is to move the letter file out of My Music and into My Pictures. So …

3

Letter to bank manager requesting a loan icon

Right-click the icon, hold down the mouse button and drag the file icon into the My Documents window. Point at the My Pictures icon and, when it becomes highlighted, release the mouse button.

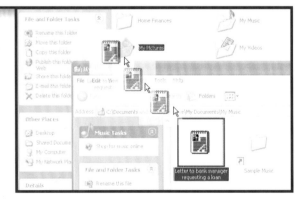

④

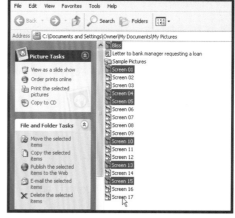

Move Here

This time, click Move Here on the pop-up menu. The letter file disappears from the My Music folder and now lives in My Pictures. To finish, close both of the open windows. Just to be clear here: copying a file to a new location does not affect the original file – you simply end up with two exact copies of the same file in different folders. When you move a file, the original is permanently removed from its original location.

Copying multiple files

We've been working with single files and folders here but you can copy or move several all at the same time. You just have to make sure that they are all selected before you begin the operation.

①

To select multiple files and sub-folders within a folder, open the folder in My Documents, switch to List view (see page 89), hold down the Ctrl key, and click each target file or sub-folder in turn

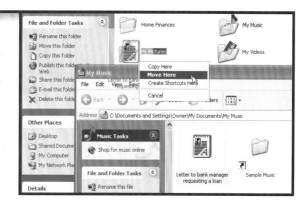

②

To select all files and sub-folders within a folder, click the first file or sub-folder on the list, hold down the Shift key, and click the last file or sub-folder.

Now the selected files behave like a single unit. Try copying or moving them using one of the methods described above. When dragging-and-dropping, simply click on any one file or folder within the selected group and the whole lot will move as one, a little like a stack of playing cards in Solitaire.

WINDOWS XP

Working with drives

Earlier, we discussed drives in the context of hardware. Now let's put them to work. We'll assume here that your computer has four drives: a hard disk drive (that's a definite), a floppy drive, a CD-RW drive and a DVD drive.

Using My Computer

On the Desktop, you'll find an icon for My Computer. Double-click it now.

 *My Computer icon*

Here we see our four drives. Note that each is assigned a drive letter (appended with a colon). This is how Windows tells one drive from another. In this case, we have:

● Floppy disk drive – A:
● Hard disk drive (labelled Local Disk) – C:
● DVD drive – D:
● CD-RW drive – E:

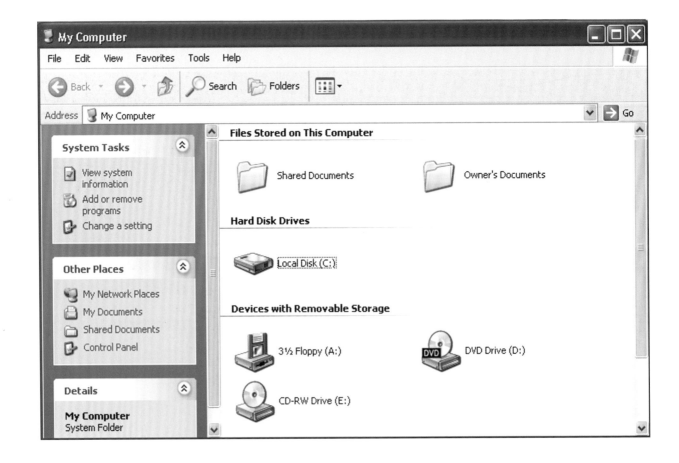

Now, the floppy drive is always A: and the hard disk drive always C:, but your CD-RW and DVD drives might be labelled the other way around depending upon how your system has been set up. It matters not: just bear in mind that each drive has its own, unique letter.

If your computer is fitted with a memory card reader, you may see several more drives in My Computer, each corresponding to the memory card formats that the reader can accept. If you have a plug-in USB 'flash' drive, it will also show up as a drive while it is plugged in but not otherwise. Similarly a digital camera can show up as a drive.

Your computer may also appear to have more than one hard disk drive, either because it physically has two or more drives or because the sole C: drive as been 'partitioned' into two or more chunks. These are not physically distinct drives but rather a way of telling Windows to treat each chunk as if it is a separate device. The most common purpose for a partitioned drive is to keep essential rescue data in a safe location. If all goes horribly wrong and you have to restore your computer to the way it looked when you first brought it home from the shop, you have the opportunity to use a rescue CD (this will have been supplied with your computer). This CD looks for the information on the partitioned drive and uses it to make repairs. Because this information is not

stored on C: drive, the chances of you having lost, deleted, overwritten or corrupted it are much slimmer than they would be otherwise, so the chances of a successful repair are greater.

To see the files and folders stored on a drive, double-click its icon in My Computer. If there is no floppy, CD or DVD in the drive, Windows will return an error message; otherwise, you can view and open its contents.

Hard disk drive. Of all the drives, the hard disk is by far the most important. Essentially, it 'is' your computer – home to Windows, programs and files. You *read data from* the hard disk drive every time you launch a program or perform a task; and you *save data to* the hard disk drive whenever you save a file. Just as with the My Documents window, you can use the View menu to work with files in different ways (*see below*). In fact, you can get to your files and folders using either My Documents or My Computer; they are entirely complementary.

My Computer lets you view the innards of your computer. Here we see one CD drive, four hard drives (in reality, four hard drive partitions, where D: is the rescue partition) and four removable drives corresponding to memory card readers.

CD-RW drive. We'll look at installing software from a CD-ROM disc on page 102 but for now let's take advantage of Windows XP's built-in *CD burning* capability. This lets you treat a recordable (or rewriteable) CD just like a floppy disk – but one with about 500 times the capacity for file storage.

Note: in this exercise, change E: to the drive letter that corresponds to your CD-RW drive.

①

🖱 *My Computer icon*

🖱 *E: icon*

🖱 *Properties*

🖱 *Recording*

🖱 *Enable CD recording on this drive*

🖱 *Apply*

🖱 *OK*

Here, we are simply setting up the drive to act as a CD recorder. This option, located in the Advanced tab of the Properties menu, may already be enabled on your computer but, if not, check it here.

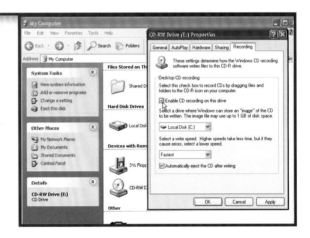

②

🖱 *Take no action*

🖱 *OK*

Now pop a blank CD-R disc in the CD-RW drive. Push the button on the drive to open the tray, lay the disc flat on the tray printed- or label-side up (plain silver-side down), and push the button to close the tray. Windows will recognise what's happening and ask for instructions. Click Take no action and close the pop-up window by clicking OK.

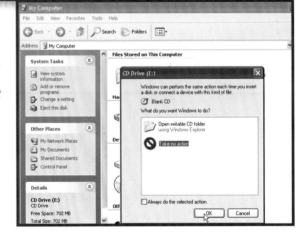

② **QUICK Q & A**

Can I make copies of my programs with my CD-RW drive? Probably. But you may be in serious trouble with the copyright cops if discovered. There is a grey area in the law which lets you make a single copy of any program specifically and exclusively for backup purposes but, if in doubt, just hang on to the original installation disc and don't risk any accusation of piracy.

3

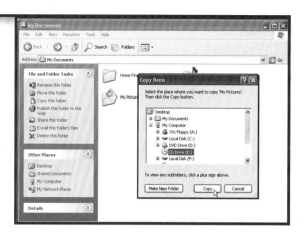

- My Documents icon
- My Pictures icon
- Copy this folder
- E:
- Copy

Open My Documents and select the My Pictures folder with a click. Now click Copy this folder option in the left pane. In the pop-up window, select the CD-RW drive (E:) and click Copy. What we're doing here is copying the entire contents of My Pictures to the CD-R disc. You could equally drag-and-drop the files as described earlier.

4

Now, for reasons too complicated to dwell upon, it is not in fact possible for Windows to copy files directly to a CD-R disc without a further step. The target files are copied on the fly to a holding, or 'staging', area. This gives you a chance to select more files to burn to the CD later: just keep copying them to the drive as in Step 3. In the meantime, when you click the Copy button, up pops a bubble inviting you to burn the files straight away. Ignore this and wait for it to disappear. Next time around, you could click the bubble to take a shortcut to Step 5 but let's go the long way around here.

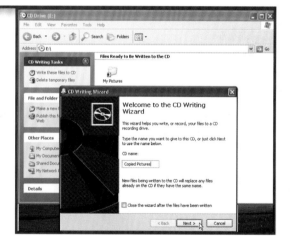

5

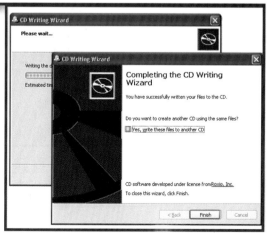

- E: icon
- Write these files to CD
- Copied Pictures
- Next

Close My Documents, open My Computer and double-click the E: icon. Now you can see the files and folders awaiting burning in the main window pane – in this case, My Pictures. Click Write these files to CD option in the left pane. In the pop-up window, give the CD a meaningful name – Copied Pictures, for example – and click Next.

6

- Finish

Windows now goes to work and burns the files onto the CD-R disc. When the process completes, click the Finish button. Now that the files have been copied, you can read them in this or any other computer's CD-ROM, CD-RW or DVD drive.

You can add more files to a CD-R disc in several different burning 'sessions' until it is full. However, each session wastes around 14MB of storage space – it's an unavoidable overhead – so it's better to add files to the staging area as you go along (see Step 4 above) and then burn the lot in a single session (Step 5).

DVD recording

Unfortunately, Windows XP doesn't allow you to record data directly onto DVD discs. However, you should find that your computer comes with some basic CD/DVD software that allows you to record to DVD just as easily as to CD. The advantage is that DVDs have a much higher capacity than CDs so you can get many more files on a single disc. Your software may also enable you to turn home movies into fully-fledged DVDs and watch them on your TV. However, this requires a bit of specialist knowledge. We recommend the *Haynes Digital Video Manual* for guidance.

You'll need specialist software for advanced recording onto CD or DVD.

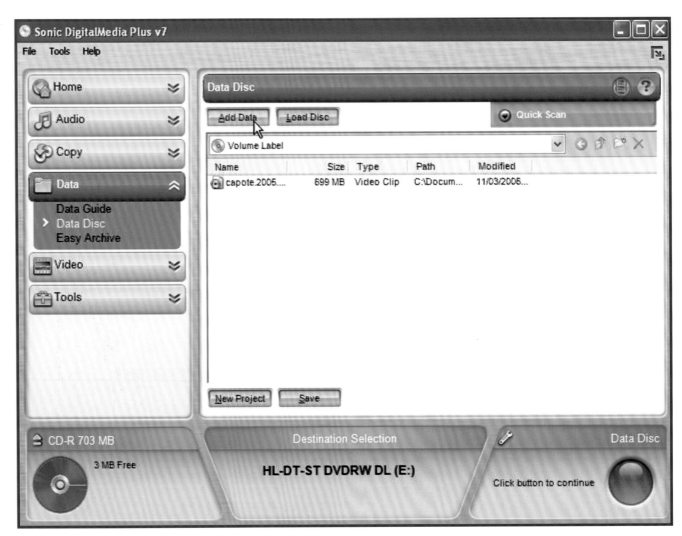

USB drives

USB 'flash' or 'pen' or 'keyring' drives are tiny solid-state (no moving parts) drives that you plug into any USB port on any computer. You can usually copy files to and from such a drive without any software installation because it appears in Windows as if it were a hard disk drive. USB drives are much faster and easier to work with than CDs or DVDs and, in our opinion, a must-have investment for quick backups. Capacities range from a few Megabytes to a few Gigabytes, with prices rising accordingly.

Copying images from a digital camera to your computer

With digital cameras ubiquitous, you'll doubtless want to transfer your images onto your computer in order to save, tweak and print them. Here's how.

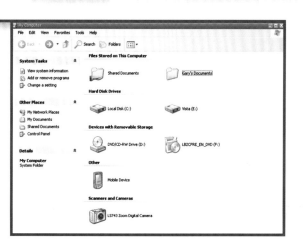

Plug one end of the camera's USB cable into the camera and the other into a USB port on your PC. Open My Computer, switch the camera on and after a few seconds, you should see it appear under Scanners and Cameras in the My Computer window. Double-click the camera icon to open it.

As you can see, Windows treats your camera's memory like any other drive or folder: you can view a list, icons or little thumbnails of the images, and you can copy the images to your PC by dragging and dropping them. The easiest way to do this is to open a second My Computer window.

Keep the first window – the one with your pictures – open and in the second window, navigate to the folder where you want to store your images. In this screenshot we're just using the My Pictures subfolder within My Documents. Return to your pictures, use the mouse to highlight the ones you want, and then drag them over the window where you want to drop them.

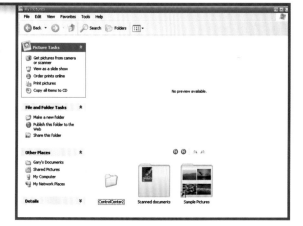

Windows will now copy your images from the camera to your computer. In our screenshot, we're having a look at the pictures that we've just copied to our PC. Unless you delete them manually the original images will remain stored in your camera's memory or on its memory card as well as on your PC.

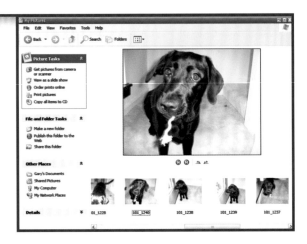

Because Windows treats your digital camera as if it were any other storage device, you can erase all the images on your camera from within Windows. There are two ways to do this: manually, by selecting the images and then dragging them to the recycle bin, or quickly, by clicking the 'Delete All Pictures...' option in the left-hand panel.

You don't need your camera to copy pictures to Windows: invest in a cheap USB card reader and you can plug the memory card straight into your PC – which is handy if, like us, you tend to lose or damage cables. Simply put the card into the card reader, put the reader into a spare USB port, and the memory card will appear in Windows Explorer as a new removable drive.

7

To view the contents of the memory card, double-click its icon in My Computer. You won't see the photos immediately, though: most cameras store their images in a folder called DCIM, which is short for 'Digital Camera Images'. Double-click the DCIM folder to see its contents.

8

Many digital cameras try to keep their photos as organised as possible, and our Kodak is no exception: rather than dumping all our images in one place, it uses a separate subfolder within the DCIM folder for each day's worth of shots. To see the contents of a subfolder, just double-click it.

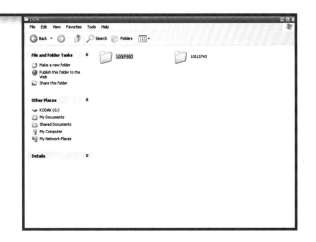

9

And here are our photos. As before, you can copy the pictures to your PC by dragging and dropping, or if you prefer you can use a program such as Picasa to import and organise them for you.

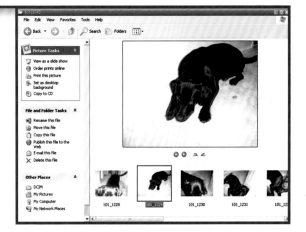

PART 3 Working with programs

So far, we've worked exclusively with and within Windows. However, for all its games, features and built-in mini-programs like WordPad and Paint, remember that Windows is 'only' an operating system for your computer. To make the most of your hardware, you'll need some application software proper. In fact, your computer supplier almost certainly supplied a program or two as part of the deal.

Now, we can't begin to cover the ins and outs of all the different programs out there but we can show you a standard software installation and removal procedure.

Installing a program

To install a program means to copy its files from a CD-ROM or DVD-ROM to your computer's hard disk drive so you can use the program whenever you like without further recourse to the disc. However, some really weighty programs, particularly encyclopaedias, do keep a lot of the *multimedia* material on the disc as an alternative to clogging up your hard disk with large files that you seldom need. In such cases, you must keep the disc in the drive while the program is running.

We're going to install Microsoft Works Suite 2002 in this example – a collection of programs that includes Word, the popular word processor.

QUICK Q & A

Should I always buy a DVD-ROM version of a new program instead of CD-ROM?
Yes, providing it's no more expensive and your computer has a DVD drive. Thanks to DVD's greater capacity, it should save you shuffling between multiple CD-ROMs while you work or play.

Close any programs currently running on your computer and pop the program's installation disc in the CD-RW drive (if it's a CD-ROM) or DVD-ROM drive (if it's a DVD). The installation program should start automatically after a few seconds. In this case, we have a choice of how to proceed. We'd suggest that you always plump for the 'typical' option. Alternatively . . .

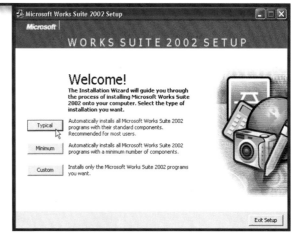

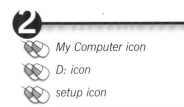

My Computer icon

D: icon

setup icon

If, however, nothing happens when you insert the disc, first ensure that you've put it into the drive the right way up (i.e. label up, shiny-side down). If there's still no action, open My Computer, double-click the icon for the drive that contains the disc (D: here), switch to List view (see page 89), and look for a file named setup. Double-click it to kick-start the installation. Alternatively . . .

Start   *Add New Programs*

Control Panel   *CD or Floppy*

Add or Remove   *Next*
Programs icon
                                           Finish

This is another alternative to try if the installation procedure does not begin automatically. Windows searches your floppy and CD/DVD drives for the necessary files and launches installation itself. Again, be sure that the disc is already in its drive.

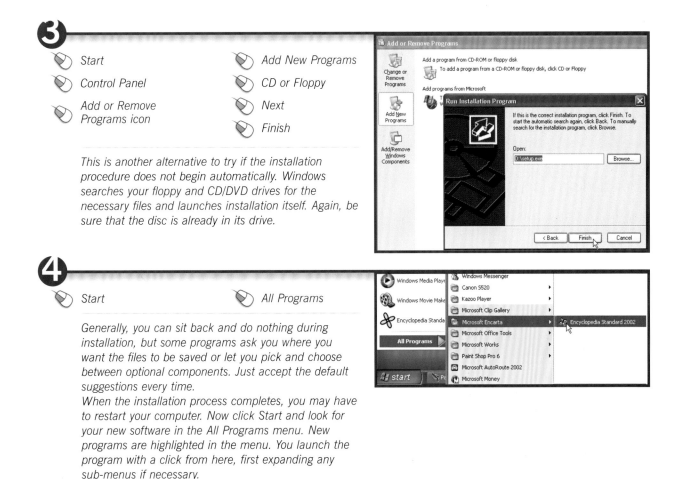

Start   *All Programs*

Generally, you can sit back and do nothing during installation, but some programs ask you where you want the files to be saved or let you pick and choose between optional components. Just accept the default suggestions every time.
When the installation process completes, you may have to restart your computer. Now click Start and look for your new software in the All Programs menu. New programs are highlighted in the menu. You launch the program with a click from here, first expanding any sub-menus if necessary.

I Agree

*If you are presented with a **user licence** when you first run a program, read the terms and conditions carefully (you'll discover that you're not allowed to make copies and flog them at a car boot sale, for example) and click Agree or Accept. If you disagree or refuse to accept its terms, the program will not run.*

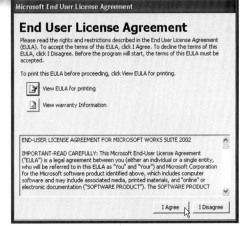

Product key

In this example, we are also prompted for the product key the first time we run Word. Also known as a security code or serial number, this ostensibly guarantees that you own a legitimate copy of the program (rather then one bought at a car boot sale). The code will be printed on the CD/DVD box or in the manual or on a paper insert in the box, or somewhere. Enter the code exactly as you see it, respecting the use of upper and lower case, dashes and spaces. You may also be invited to register the program with the developer in order to receive free updates and upgrades. This can normally be done over the internet, so perhaps wait until the next section!
*NB. Word comes with Microsoft's **Product Activation** feature, just like Windows XP (see Glossary).*

Uninstalling a program

There will come a time when you no longer have a need for one or more of your programs. Now, it generally does no harm to let redundant software rest undisturbed on your hard disk. However, hard disks have a finite capacity and even today, when they have hundreds of *Gigabytes* of storage space, you may eventually need to free up room to install some new programs. Or you may install a program that you simply don't get along with.

Once uninstalled, a program can no longer be run on your computer. You can always *re*install it, of course, providing you still have the original CD-ROM or DVD.

One point to note: uninstalling a program does not *usually* remove any files that you created yourself with it. Uninstalling Word, for instance, will not delete your letter files. However, because programs often use proprietary file formats, you may find that you can no longer access your files without the original program. The moral of which is: take care, and use non-proprietary file formats wherever possible.

QUICK Q & A
Q: Why are software boxes so big and bulky when there's nothing inside but a CD-ROM and a lot of fresh air?
A: They look good on superstore shelves.

📀 *Start*

📀 *All Programs*

📀 *[find program]*

📀 *Uninstall*

Some, but by no means all, programs can be uninstalled straight from the Start Menu. If present, the option will always be tucked away in a sub-menu. Click it and follow the directions. Alternatively ...

2

🖱 *Start*

🖱 *Control Panel*

🖱 *Add or Remove Programs icon*

🖱 *Change or Remove Programs*

🖱 *[select program]*

🖱 *Change/Remove*

🖱 *Yes*

The Add or Remove Programs window shows you a list of all the software installed on your computer, and you simply highlight the target program and click the Change/Remove button. (If there are separate Change and Remove buttons, click Remove.) Confirm your intentions in the next window by clicking Yes.

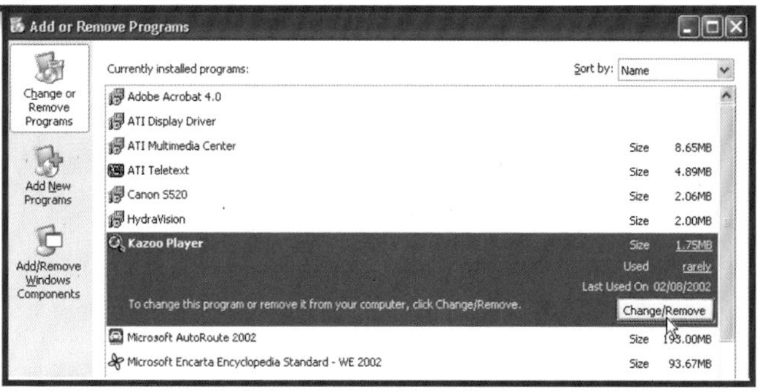

3

🖱 *Start*

🖱 *Next*

You may see a window similar to this, in which case check the Remove option, click Next and follow further directions.

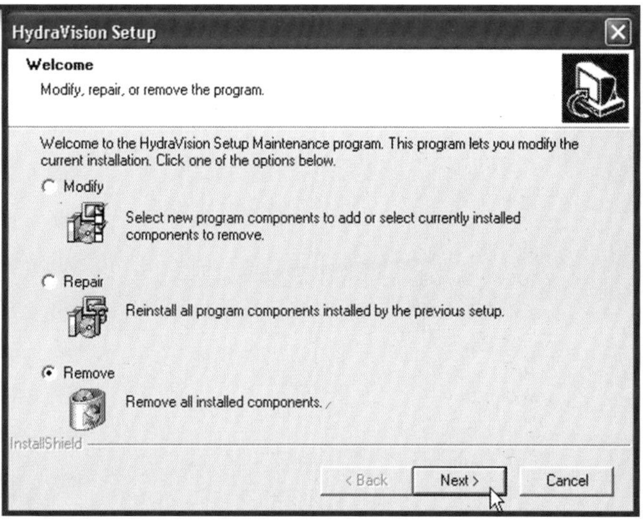

QUICK Q & A

Q: I've just bought this expensive new program and I can't find the manual!
A: A sign of the times, we're afraid. Manuals are now routinely supplied in electronic form, which means there's a file somewhere on the installation disc. As often

as not, this will be an Adobe Acrobat file, which can only be opened and read with a program called Acrobat Reader. A copy of this will be provided on the disc along with the manual (or, if not, you can download it from www.adobe.com).

Unfreezing your computer

Windows is designed for multi-tasking (i.e. doing several things at once). This means that you can easily run two, three or more programs at the same time – perhaps an e-mail program, a web browser, a word processor and a music player.

However, there are certain limitations. Without getting too technical, the number of programs and tasks you can perform simultaneously depends on how much memory your computer has and, to a lesser extent, the speed of its processor. If you try to do *too* much, everything will slow to a crawl and you'll spend more time drumming your fingers on your desk waiting for windows to open than typing on your keyboard. In the worst case, your computer may actually 'freeze'. No matter what you click, nothing happens: the screen display refuses to change and your computer is effectively lifeless. What to do?

Well, you have two options. First, press and hold the Ctrl + Alt + Delete keys on your keyboard simultaneously. This launches a window called Windows Task Manager. As soon as it appears, release all three keys.

Task Manager has several tabs but you're interested in Applications. Here you'll see a list of all programs currently running on your computer. If any program is marked as 'Not Responding' in the Status, that's your culprit right there. Select the program and click End Task. Windows will now close this – *and only this* – program, and you should be able to use your computer as normal again. The downside is that any open file within that program will also close, and so you'll lose the changes you made since the last time you saved it. We'll come to that in the very next section.

If Task Manager can't resolve your troubles and your computer is absolutely frozen, there is another option – but this one is strictly for Emergency Use Only. Press the reset button on the system unit. This bypasses the usual shutdown procedure and immediately turns your computer off and on again. Here, too, you'll lose any unsaved files, and this time it affects *all* open programs. Windows may also launch a **diagnostic utility** before it restarts.

There's no need to panic if a program freezes your computer – Task Manager can usually save the day.

The reset button really is the last resort.

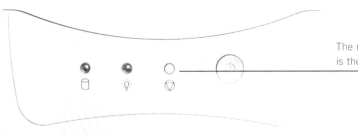

MESH

The all-important Save button

If there's one lesson that all computer owners learn the hard way, it is this: losing your work is a nightmare. Be it a power failure, a system freeze or an accidental click on the wrong button, there's nothing like watching a critical file or project disappear forever to make you wish you'd never set eyes on your hardware.

But it needn't be so! Barring the most extreme misadventure, any file saved to your hard disk is safe. Back on page 83, we looked at how to save a new file using the Save As command. This same procedure applies in virtually all programs: you give each new file a name and save it. However, the critical thing – the really, *really* critical thing – is remembering to save your work *as you go along*.

When you first save a file, it is allocated a slice of hard disk space. However, the moment you open and change that file in any way – add or delete a word or a sentence or an image, or change the formatting, or do anything whatsoever – the open file and the saved file are no longer identical. The open file is held in a kind of flux while you work, and is vulnerable to all sorts of mishap. This is why it is vital to save your work continually. The idea is simply to minimise the period between your last save and the moment catastrophe strikes – and, since you never know when catastrophe is going to strike, this means saving your work *frequently*. We would suggest that once every couple of minutes is a good target.

How do you save your work? In almost every case, you will find a Save button on your program's Toolbar (it often looks like a floppy disk). Failing this, click File on the Menu Bar and look for the Save command.

There are some exceptions, however. E-mail programs, for instance, automatically save incoming messages without the need for you to do anything.

Alternatively, many programs allow you to use a keyboard shortcut: pressing the Ctrl + S keys simultaneously has the same effect as clicking Save.

Every time you save a file, the file on your hard disk is overwritten with the open version. If you wish to avoid this, use the Save As command instead, and save the open file with a new name. Thus you might open your 'Letter to the bank manager requesting a loan' and save it immediately as, say, 'Loan agreement details'. Now you can use the original file as a useful template without in any way affecting it.

Save your work-in-progress with a button, a menu command or a keyboard shortcut.

What does what?

The range of programs is truly vast, from free utilities to super-expensive video editing suites. Moreover, while you probably know a few of the big software names, like Microsoft, there is tremendous competition in most markets. We would strongly advise that you research any potential purchase thoroughly, as no two programs are ever quite identical. What might appear to be a minor weakness in one slightly cheaper program may, in fact, make it wholly unsuitable for your intentions; on the other hand, you can often save a good deal of money by opting for software that has a lower specification but still does all you need of it.

There is also a tremendous degree of cross-over among genres. A word processor, for instance, is perfect for writing letters (and computer manuals) but can also handle figures and even basic design and illustrative work. Don't splash out on new software if your existing programs can handle your needs.

Each new program involves another learning curve. However, Windows encourages a roughly standard interface, or appearance, so it's often possible to work out the basics fairly quickly.

These screens show very different types of program – one is designed for editing text; the other for editing images – but note the similarities. Both have a Title Bar, a Menu Bar, a number of Toolbars and a large central working area. In short, you click things – buttons, menus, icons – to make stuff happen.

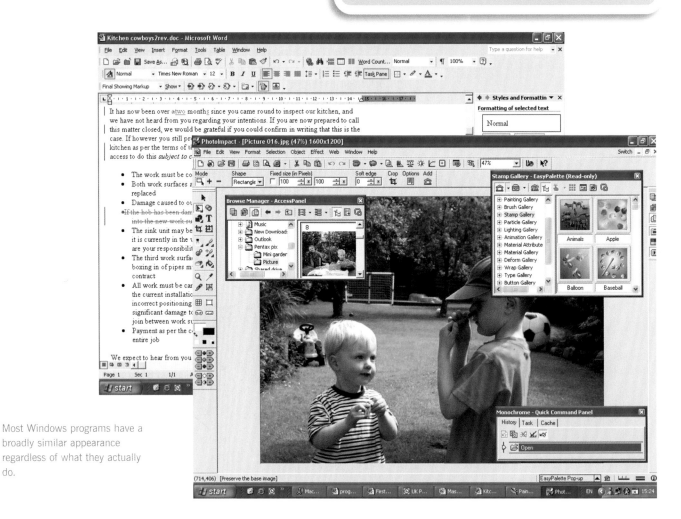

Most Windows programs have a broadly similar appearance regardless of what they actually do.

Here is a very rough, ready and by no means exhaustive
guide to popular types of program and what they do
best:

Program type	What can you do with it?
Antivirus	Prevent potentially harmful viruses from damaging your computer.
CAD (Computer Aided Design)	Design products digitally on a computer.
CD burning	Record audio, video and data compilations onto CDs.
Database	Collate and manage complex and/or large quantities of data.
DTP (Desktop Publishing)	Design documents and projects using text and images.
E-mail	Send, receive and manage e-mail messages.
Financial management	Keep tabs on your incomings and outgoings.
Firewall	Protect your computer from internet *hackers*.
Games	Computer games range from child-friendly educational tools to blood-thirsty shoot-'em-ups.
Image editor	Edit and enhance digital pictures imported from a scanner or a digital camera.
Instant messenger	Exchange text messages across the internet in real time.
Multimedia player	Play music and videos on your computer.
Office suite	A compendium of business tools, typically including a word processor, spreadsheet, database, e-mail and PIM.
PIM (Personal Information Manager)	Keep track of your contacts with an address book, diary and calendar.
Presentation	Create professional presentations, particularly suited to sales proposals.
Project management	Control a complex project from conception to completion.
Reference	General and specific research – dictionary, encyclopaedia, atlas, etc.
Sound editor	Record and edit digital sound files, including musical instruments.
Speech recognition	Train your computer to recognise your voice (well, up to a point).
Spreadsheet	Perform advanced calculations with figures laid out in rows and columns.
System utilities	Maintain and trouble-shoot your computer at a sub-Windows level.
Video editor	Turn raw camcorder footage into a polished movie.
Web browser	Visit web pages and sites on the internet.
Web editor	Design and build your own web pages.
Word processor	Create and edit text-based documents.

PART ⑤ The best programs in the world ... ever

From managing money to creating your own DVD discs, your PC's potential is almost limitless – provided you have the right software. Some of that software is already in Windows (or may have come bundled with your computer), but for some jobs you will need to download or buy additional programs. In this section we'll discover the things most PC owners will want to do, the tools that come bundled with Windows and the programs that can help.

I want to ... make my own CDs

If you want to burn files to CD, you can do it from within Windows: just stick a blank CD into your CD burner and a window pops up asking what you want to do. If you then choose 'open writable CD folder' you can then add files to the CD by dragging and dropping them into the folder.

If you want to make music CDs, for example by turning MP3 music files into a CD you can play in the car, then you can use Windows Media Player to do that. However, we prefer Apple's free iTunes program, which you can get from **www.apple.com/itunes**

For really advanced CD burning such as creating photo or video CDs, software CDs or DVDs, we'd recommend a dedicated burning program such as Easy Media Creator (**www.roxio.com**) or Nero Burning ROM (**www.nero.com**). Expect to pay around £60.

Although you can burn CDs from within Windows, dedicated CD burning software such as Easy Media Creator can make music, photo and video CDs or DVDs.

Many internet videos use a technology called DivX, and won't work in standard video software – but you can download a free DivX player from **www.divx.com**.

I want to ... play music and movies

We've already mentioned Windows Media Player and Apple's iTunes. While the programs work in slightly different ways they're both very good at organising and playing music and movie files. However, if you want to watch DVDs (and didn't get a DVD viewing program with your computer) then we'd recommend WinDVD. This turns any Windows PC into a DVD player. At the time of writing WinDVD sells for around £25.

If you fancy downloading video from the internet, you'll be able to do so via Windows Media Player or Apple's iTunes – but you might find that some online videos won't play with either program. That's because online video comes in several different formats, and one of the most popular is called DivX. You can download free DivX player software from **www.divx.com**.

I want to ...
organise and share my digital photos

With a Windows PC you can simply connect your digital camera and copy the pictures to your hard disk, but there's a good range of software that takes things up a notch. One of our favourites is Picasa (**www.picasa.google.com**), a free photo program that not only helps you organise your pictures but also gives you the tools to change them.

For more ambitious jobs such as photo editing and retouching, we'd recommend Adobe's Photoshop Elements (£47 from **www.adobe.co.uk**) or Paint Shop Pro (around £60 from **www.corel.com**). Both programs are incredibly powerful and enable you to fix dodgy snaps, transform your pictures and even create new images by using bits from several different photos. Be warned – they're very addictive.

Programs such as Adobe's Photoshop Elements can help you organise, enhance, fix and edit your digital images and photographs.

I want to ... make my own movies

Windows includes a copy of Windows Movie Maker, which is designed to help you edit camcorder footage. Unfortunately we don't think it's very good. We much prefer Adobe's Premiere Elements (£45 from **www.adobe.co.uk**). This nifty little program turns your PC into a movie studio, where you can edit your camcorder clips, add special effects, titles and credits, replace the soundtrack and burn the finished masterpiece to DVD. Ten years ago you'd have needed a computer the size of a house and a wallet the size of Wales to do the same thing.

For around £45 you can turn your PC into a Hollywood-style video studio. Programs such as Premiere Elements even enable you to add special effects.

I want to ...
talk to my friends and family online

There are lots of free chat programs available, including Yahoo! Messenger (**www.yahoo.co.uk**), AOL Instant Messenger (**www.aol.co.uk**) and MSN Messenger (**www.msn.co.uk**). However, they can't talk to one another – so if you're on MSN Messenger and a friend uses Yahoo! Messenger, you won't be able to chat. You can solve the problem by using a multi-chat client, which is a chat program that can connect to several different services at the same time. Our favourite chat program is the free Trillian Basic, which you can download from **www.trillian.cc**.

Chat software enables you to talk in real-time to others, but they're also capable of swapping files, video chat and in the case of Yahoo! Messenger, making phone calls from your PC.

I want to ... manage my money

Windows doesn't include any money management tools, but you can get very good financial software for very little outlay. Microsoft Money (£22, **ww.microsoft.co.uk**) is a superb tool for organising and keeping an eye on your personal finances, and it integrates with many online banking services too.

For small businesses, the market leaders are Sage Instant Accounts (£90, **www.sage.com**) and QuickBooks (£109, **www.intuit.com**). Both programs take the tedium out of invoicing, income and expenditure, and they can also help make tax time less terrifying.

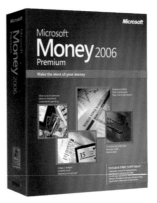

Microsoft Money is very easy to use, integrates with many online banking systems and can help you keep track of your spending.

I want to ... get organised

If your PC came with a copy of Microsoft Office then you've already got Outlook, a heavy-duty e-mail program that doubles as a calendar, to-do list and project management package. However, if you don't have Office, just head for the internet instead. Google Calendar (**www.calendar.google.com**) is a handy online calendar that you can use to manage your own time, or to publish events calendars for clubs and other organisations. It's free, too.

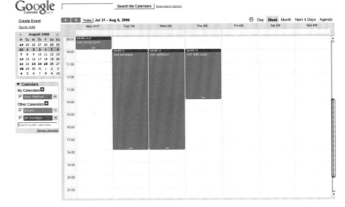

Google's free Calendar service can help organise your life, and you can also use it to publish public calendars for clubs or venues.

I want to ...
make leaflets, posters and newsletters

It's possible to create fairly complicated documents in any word processor, but for best results you'd be better off with dedicated Desktop Publishing (DTP) software. One of the best ones is Serif's PagePlus, which comes in two versions: PagePlus 11, which is a heavyweight DTP package and costs around £70; and PagePlus SE, which is a simpler version and which is completely free of charge. You can download PagePlus SE – and other free programs – from **www.freeserifsoftware.com**.

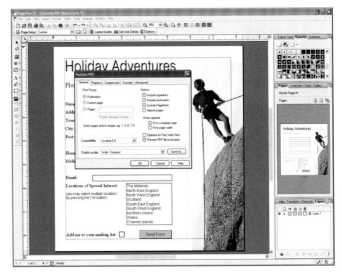

Although you can create complex documents with standard word processing software, dedicated desktop publishing packages such as PagePlus offer powerful publishing features.

I want to ... get the best from the internet

Although Windows comes with a free web browser (Internet Explorer) and a free e-mail program (Outlook Express), there are better options available. For browsing, we'd recommend Firefox (**www.mozilla.com/firefox**), a safe, secure browser that you can customise so that it looks and works the way you want it to, and for e-mail it's worth checking out Thunderbird (**www.mozilla.com/thunderbird**), which is the e-mail equivalent of Firefox. They're excellent programs and offer much more power than the programs you get with Windows.

Instead of using Outlook Express, try Thunderbird as your e-mail program: it's very powerful and more secure than Microsoft's basic e-mail program.

I want to ...
protect my kids from dodgy websites

Windows XP does include some parental control features – you'll find them by clicking Tools then Internet Options in your copy of Internet Explorer – but setting them up can be very time-consuming. Programs such as Net Nanny (**www.netnanny.com**) are a better option, because they do more than restrict the sites your kids can see: they can limit the amount of time your kids spend online, prevent them from using file sharing software, ensure that they don't give out personal information and even limit the amount of time spent playing games. Net Nanny costs £25 for a one-year licence. The program downloads updates to its blacklist every month.

While programs such as Net Nanny are undoubtedly effective, it's important to know their limits. We've been testing such software for years, and while they block the overwhelming majority of potentially offensive content it's still possible for the odd dodgy site to slip through the net – or for perfectly legitimate sites to be blocked by mistake. Such mistakes are rare but they do happen occasionally, which means that parental control software isn't perfect.

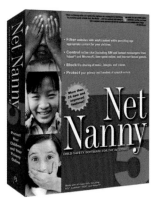

Filtering software such as Net Nanny can prevent your kids from seeing inappropriate content and can also limit the time they spend online.

Internet security suites can protect you from all kinds of nasties including spyware and viruses.

I want to ... keep my system safe

There are lots of nasties on the internet, and unfortunately almost all of them affect Windows. Windows XP does include a firewall program which can stop malicious programs getting onto your computer and Windows Update can download fixes for any security issues within Windows itself; but for strong security it's a good idea to get some dedicated security software such as Norton internet Security (**www.symantec.com**), McAfee internet Security (www.mcafee.com) or ZoneAlarm Security Suite (**www.zonelabs.com**). Security suites range in price from around £30 to £60, and they keep your PC safe from viruses and other malicious software. In many cases they also include features that are designed to protect your confidential information from falling into the wrong hands, together with Net Nanny-style parental control features.

You can also improve your computer's security by changing the software you use. We've already mentioned Firefox and Thunderbird, the free web browser and e-mail program; both programs suffer from fewer malicious attacks than Internet Explorer and Outlook Express, and in the case of Firefox you can also install additional tools – called Extensions – that block online annoyances such as noisy adverts.

4

PART **4** # The internet

E-mail, websites, online shopping, instant chat, community groups, research, online gaming, file-sharing, live news and entertainment updates, streaming video and radio … all this and much, much more is possible with your computer. In fact, there's every chance that you bought a computer precisely because you want to be part of this global communications network called the internet.

In this section, we will discuss how to get online in the first place and then spend a little time looking at using a web browser and an e-mail program. We'll also practise downloading a file, and round up with a touch of essential paranoia.

PART 4 Getting online

Getting onto the internet is easy: you've already got a PC, so all you need now is an internet connection. For that, you'll need two things: an account with an Internet Service Provider (ISP), and something to connect your PC to your phone line.

There are two kinds of internet access: dial-up and broadband. Until a few years ago dial-up was the only kind of internet access you could get, but broadband is now widely available and very affordable. It's also much, much better.

Dial-up internet connections use fairly old technology, and as a result the connections are slow: downloading a single MP3 music file might take five minutes or more. Even the slowest broadband services are much, much faster than that, so for example you could download an entire album over broadband in less time than a dial-up user could download a single song. If you want to download music or movies, share your digital photos or play online games, broadband is a better bet – particularly now that entry-level services cost around £15 per month for unlimited access.

The other difference between dial-up and broadband internet access is equipment. Most PCs come with a modem, which enables you to connect your PC to the phone line and access the internet via a dial-up account, but those modems don't work with broadband. However, most ISPs will provide you with all the equipment you need when you sign up for a broadband account.

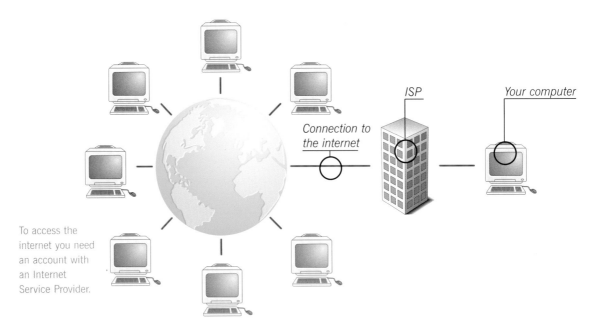

To access the internet you need an account with an Internet Service Provider.

Broadband comes in two main flavours: ADSL, which is delivered via your BT phone line, and cable broadband, which uses cable networks from firms such as NTL.

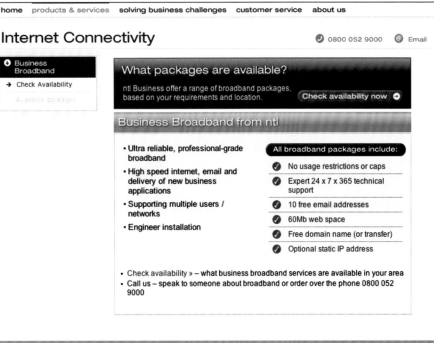

Choosing a broadband service

There are two kinds of broadband: ADSL, which uses the phone network, and cable, which uses cable TV firms' networks. The main difference between the two technologies is availability: if you can get cable TV you can probably get cable broadband; if you can't, you probably can't. Similarly if you've got a BT phone then you can probably get ADSL, although if you're in a rural area you might not be able to get the very fastest ADSL services. That's because ADSL needs you to be fairly close to the local phone exchange – within a couple of kilometres – in order to deliver its maximum speeds.

When you're choosing broadband there are four things to consider. The first is, of course, price, but you also need to choose the speed of your connection, whether it's capped or uncapped, and whether you want the Internet Service Provider to provide the hardware or choose it yourself.

What do the speeds mean?

Despite what some firms' ads would have you believe, connections slower than 512Kbps (Kilobits Per Second) aren't broadband – although a 150Kbps service is certainly faster than a dial-up connection, which runs out of steam at around 40Kbps. However, to get the full benefits of broadband you'll need 512Kbps or more.

For a long time 512Kbps was the fastest connection you could get, but as the technology has improved speeds have increased. Most firms offer affordable 1MBps (1,000Kbps) and 2MBps connections, while others are even faster: 8MB, 10MB and even 22MB in some cities. The cheapest services are usually the

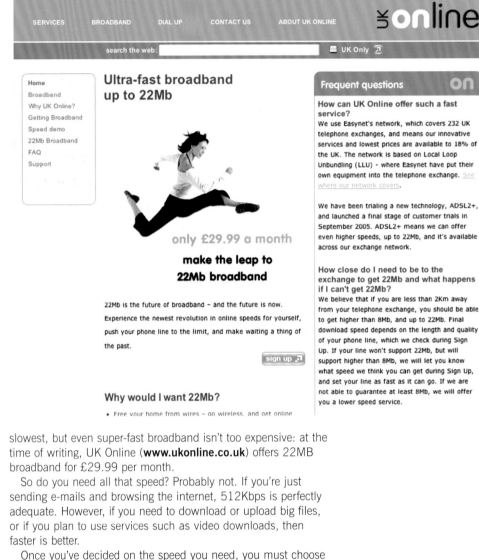

slowest, but even super-fast broadband isn't too expensive: at the time of writing, UK Online (**www.ukonline.co.uk**) offers 22MB broadband for £29.99 per month.

So do you need all that speed? Probably not. If you're just sending e-mails and browsing the internet, 512Kbps is perfectly adequate. However, if you need to download or upload big files, or if you plan to use services such as video downloads, then faster is better.

Once you've decided on the speed you need, you must choose an Internet Service Provider. Computer magazines regularly print 'best buy' advice. If you can get online from someone else's computer then ISPReview (**www.ispreview.co.uk**) and ADSLGuide (**www.adslguide.org.uk**) enable you to see what ISPs' customers think. Watch out for the small print in ISPs' contracts, too: most firms offer 1-month contracts, so if you're not happy you can switch – but some firms tie you into 12 or even 18-month contracts with hefty administration fees should you decide to change ISP.

To cap or not to cap?

Many firms offer the same broadband product in two versions: capped and uncapped. Uncapped is always more expensive, because it means there's no limit to how much you download. Capped services are limited, so for example Pipex's Start service (**www.solo.pipex.net**) gives you a 'usage allowance' of 1GB per month; if you want more you'll pay £2.70 for each 3GB block. A Gigabyte of data sounds like a lot, but if you're downloading big files such as digital photos or video clips then you'll quickly reach the limit.

What can **BT Broadband** do for your business ?

BT Business Broadband could save your business time and money. Whether you're looking for unlimited **UK broadband phone calls** or even extra computer help from a **'remote' IT Support Manager**, we'll make broadband work for you.
Now from **£19.99**

We tick all the boxes:

- FREE connection & FREE router ✓
- Security (firewall, email anti-virus and anti-spam) ✓
- Support (24/7 business helpdesk) ✓
- No pressure 3 month trial [1] ✓
- Unlimited UK phone calls from £14.99 per month [2] ✓

Now just choose the right Broadband package for you:

Lite: £19.99 per month (ex. VAT)

- Fast access - up to 2Mbps download speeds
- 10GB usage allowance
- Easy self-install
- Ideal for new internet users

More details ▶ Order now ▶

Single: £29.99 per month (ex. VAT)

- Fast access - up to 2Mbps download speeds
- Unlimited usage
- Easy self-install & 'IT Support Manager' offer
- Ideal for growing business

More details ▶ Order now ▶

Who supplies the hardware?

Many broadband ISPs have special offers where, if you sign up for broadband, they'll give you a free modem. That's not necessarily a bad deal, but there are limits to what your free modem can do. Such modems are typically basic USB models that aren't designed to do anything bar connect a single computer to the internet, so if you want to use your broadband connection for a network or wireless network you'd be better off supplying your own kit.

To share your broadband between PCs, you'll need a box called a router. This 'routes' network traffic, and it typically includes a connection for your phone line and then four or more ports for network connections. Wireless routers also have an antenna, which provides the signal for a wireless network.

Whether you go for a standard router or a wireless one, make sure it's the right kind of router: ADSL-compatible routers might not work with cable broadband, and vice versa. You might find that your ISP recommends a particular router and offers to sell one to you; if it does, do a quick search on a price comparison search engine such as Kelkoo (**www.kelkoo.com**) to see if you can get the same device for less money.

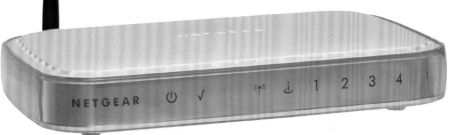

Connecting to broadband

To connect to broadband you'll need either a USB modem, which plugs into a USB port on your PC and connects to your phone line, or a router, which you connect to your PC using an Ethernet cable (so you'll need a spare Ethernet port on your PC to use it). When you sign up for broadband, your ISP will provide you with the necessary equipment; or you can buy your own from a computer shop.

Connecting a USB modem is simple: connect the modem to a spare USB port, run the installation CD, and when prompted by the software enter the username and password your ISP has provided you with. Routers are a bit more complicated, but not dramatically so – and as you'll see from this walkthrough, the principle is essentially the same. If you're using a USB modem and don't intend to share your broadband with more than one computer, you can skip this section.

1

The first step is to connect the broadband cable, which looks like a telephone cable, to the back of the router. If you're using ADSL broadband, connect the other end to a microfilter – a box that splits your phone line into two connections, one for the phone and the other for the broadband – which plugs into the phone socket. If your ISP provided you with a router, it should have supplied the microfilters too: without a microfilter you'll lose your internet connection whenever you use the phone. You need to put a microfilter on every phone point where you use a telephone.

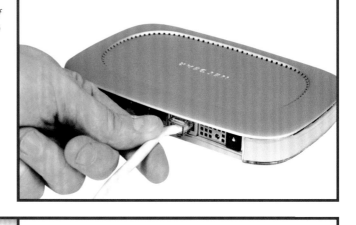

2

Now, you can connect your PC. We've already connected an Ethernet cable to the back of the PC, and it's just a matter of plugging the other end of the cable into one of the empty Ethernet ports on the back of the router.

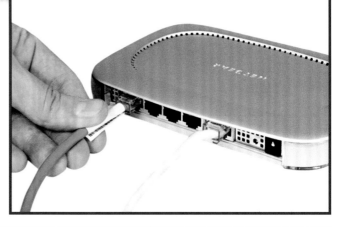

3

If you'll be sharing your broadband connection with more than one computer, you can do it with an Ethernet cable (as shown here): simply get a second cable, plug one end into the PC and plug the other end into the next available Ethernet port on the router. If you've got a wireless router and will be connecting your other devices via wireless, you can skip this step.

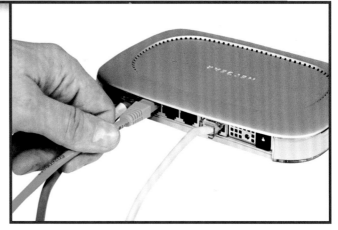

Configuring your router for broadband

Before you can use your router, you need to configure it. The good news is it's very quick and very easy to do, as we'll discover in this walkthrough.

1 Once you've connected your cables and plugged in the power cord, switch on your PC and open your web browser. To access the router configuration screen you'll need to type its address in your browser. The router manual will tell you what this address is: in this example we're using a Netgear router, and the address is http://192.168.0.1.

http://192.168.0.1

2 The router will ask for a user name and password. Once again you'll find these details in the manual. With Netgear routers the default username is 'admin' and the default password is 'password', so if you enter those details in the appropriate boxes you'll be able to access your router's control panel. Remember to change the user name and password later, or anybody will be able to change your settings!

Prompt

Enter username and password for "NETGEAR DG834GT" at 192.168.0.1

User Name:

admin

Password:

****

☑ Use Password Manager to remember this password.

Cancel   OK

3 The first thing we need to do is to configure the router to work with our broadband connection. You'll need your ISP's login details and connection settings to do this, so make sure you've got them handy before attempting this step. Once you've got the necessary details to hand, click Basic Settings in the left-hand side of the screen.

Setup Wizard

Setup

Basic Settings

ADSL Settings

Wireless Settings

4 You'll now be asked whether your connection requires a login (most do) and then for your username and password. You'll also be asked to specify the encapsulation type – your ISP will have given you this information – and to specify your internet IP address and Domain Name Server addresses. In most cases the correct options will be 'Get Dynamically from ISP' and 'Get Automatically from ISP', and your ISP will have provided the necessary numbers if that isn't the case. Finally, you need to select whether Network Address Translation should be enabled. Again, in most cases the answer is yes.

Don't worry about the various acronyms – DNS, NAT and so on. All you need to do is to ensure that the information you enter into the router control panel matches the details you've been given by your Internet Service Provider.

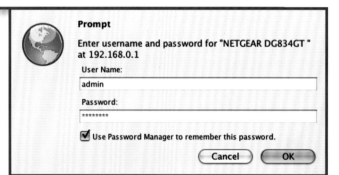

Once you've entered the details, click Apply to save them permanently. The router will now attempt to connect to your broadband connection using the details you've specified. In the case of Netgear routers, it will display a pop-up window that provides a progress report on how it's getting on. If the information you've entered is correct, after a few seconds the pop-up window will change and display the 'success page' shown here. You're up and running!

Cutting the cables

One of the best things about broadband is that you can share it using a wireless network, which makes all kinds of interesting things possible. With wireless, you can use a laptop in the garden and still access the internet, and it means you can play online games without having to drill holes through walls or run cables around your house.

Wireless standards

There are two main wireless standards: 802.11b, and 802.11g. 802.11g is much faster than 802.11b and uses slightly different technology, so a wireless card that only supports the b standard won't be able to connect to a g network. However, most wireless cards now support both standards, so look for products that are described as 802.11b/g and you'll be fine.

There's a third standard, 802.11n. This is even faster than 802.11g, and it uses a technology called MIMO – multiple inputs, multiple outputs – to improve signal strength and speed. However, at the time of writing the 802.11n standard hasn't been finalised. That hasn't stopped companies selling 802.11n hardware, but beware: until the standard has been agreed by all the main players, you might find that so-called 'pre-n' hardware doesn't work properly with other firms' 802.11n products.

If that wasn't confusing enough, some manufacturers also offer their own versions of existing standards, so for example you'll see wireless products advertised as 'Super G' that offer much faster speeds than 802.11g is supposed to deliver. Such products do work, but they only work with other products that use the same technology – so if you buy a Super G router but a standard 802.11g wireless network card, you won't get any benefit from the Super G technology.

You can add wireless network support to almost any computer. Wireless adaptors come in PCI (for installing inside desktop PCs), PC cards (for laptops, as shown here) or USB flavours.

Beware 'standards' such as Super G: they're the manufacturer's own, so if you use other firms' equipment you might not get the advertised speeds.

Configuring a wireless network

In our last walkthrough we showed you how to connect to broadband using a router. Because we've used a wireless router, we can now create a wireless network that shares the broadband between multiple computers.

Go to the router configuration screen as before, but this time click Wireless Settings. In the Name (SSID) box, choose a descriptive name for your network such as 'my home network'. Make sure that Enable Wireless Access Point and Allow Broadcast of Name (SSID) are ticked: they tell the router that it should let computers connect to it, and that it should broadcast a message that essentially says 'hello! I'm a wireless network and my name is "my home network"'.

Wireless Settings

Wireless Network
Name (SSID): my home office
Region: Europe
Channel: Auto
Mode: Auto 108Mbps

Wireless Access Point
☑ Enable Wireless Access Point
☑ Allow Broadcast of Name (SSID)
☐ Wireless Isolation
☐ Atheros eXtended Range (XR)

Wireless Station Access List (Setup Access List)

Security Options
○ Disable
◉ WEP (Wired Equivalent Privacy)
○ WPA-PSK (Wi-Fi Protected Access Pre-Shared Key)
○ WPA-802.1x

Now for some security. Click the WEP (Wired Equivalent Privacy) button to enable the WEP security system, and then choose '128 bit' from the Encryption Strength field. This makes it very difficult for people to get into your network. Now, you need to create a security key. In the Passphrase box, type any phrase you like; the router will then generate a complicated password, called a 'key', such as 9588BEF5DD4. Take a note of this number: you'll need to enter it on any computer that will use your wireless network. Click Apply to save the settings.

WEP Security Encryption
Authentication Type: Automatic
Encryption Strength: 128 bit
WEP Key
Passphrase: [ ] (Generate)
Key 1: ◉ 9588BEF5DD43D922DFA7F49355
Key 2: ○ 9588BEF5DD43D922DFA7F49355
Key 3: ○ 9588BEF5DD43D922DFA7F49355
Key 4: ○ 9588BEF5DD43D922DFA7F49355

(Apply) (Cancel)

Whenever a wireless-enabled computer is within range of your network, it will spot 'my home network' and ask if you want to connect with it. This is where the key you wrote down in step 2 matters: without it, you won't be able to connect to the network (this is a good thing because it keeps other people's computers out of your network). In this screenshot we're connecting with an Apple computer. We've entered the correct wireless key so when we click OK we'll be connected to the network.

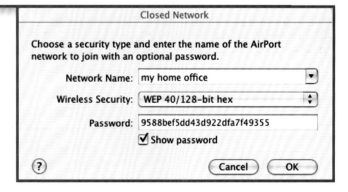

Closed Network

Choose a security type and enter the name of the AirPort network to join with an optional password.

Network Name: my home office
Wireless Security: WEP 40/128-bit hex
Password: 9588bef5dd43d922dfa7f49355
☑ Show password

(?)   (Cancel) (OK)

Connecting via dial-up

If you don't live in an area where broadband is available – or you only plan to connect to the Net from time to time, and don't fancy paying a monthly subscription – then you can still get online with a dial-up connection. Your PC probably came with a built-in modem, and as you'll see from this walkthrough it's very simple to get up and running. As with broadband, you'll need an account with an Internet Service Provider (ISP) before you can connect: in most cases they'll send you a CD that takes care of the installation for you, but some ISPs expect you to do it yourself. Here's how to do it.

Dig out the modem cable that came with your computer system. One end plugs into the 'line' socket on the modem and the other into a standard telephone socket. If there are two sockets on the modem, the second is for connecting a telephone handset, and should be clearly marked or labelled as such. Check the computer or modem manual if in doubt. Do remember that you can't use the telephone while your computer is connected to the internet. Callers will get an engaged tone.

1

- *My Network Places icon*
- *View network connections*
- *Create a new connection*
- *Next*

My Network Places is an icon on your Desktop. Look for the network connections options in the left pane. This process launches the New Connection Wizard.

New Connection Wizard

Welcome to the New Connection Wizard

This wizard helps you:

- Connect to the Internet.
- Connect to a private network, such as your workplace network.
- Set up a home or small office network.

To continue, click Next.

< Back | Next > | Cancel

2

- *Connect to the internet*
- *Next*
- *Set up my connection manually*
- *Next*
- *Connect using a dial-up modem*
- *Next*

Here, you simply make selections from the Wizard's suggestions and keep clicking the Next button.

New Connection Wizard

Internet Connection
How do you want to connect to the Internet?

○ **Connect using a dial-up modem**
This type of connection uses a modem and a regular or ISDN phone line.

○ **Connect using a broadband connection that requires a user name and password**
This is a high-speed connection using either a DSL or cable modem. Your ISP may refer to this type of connection as PPPoE.

○ **Connect using a broadband connection that is always on**
This is a high-speed connection using either a cable modem, DSL or LAN connection. It is always active, and doesn't require you to sign in.

< Back | Next > | Cancel

3

- *[ISP name]*
- *Next*

Type in the name of your ISP. In this case, it happens to be Freeserve.

New Connection Wizard

Connection Name
What is the name of the service that provides your Internet connection?

Type the name of your ISP in the following box.

ISP Name

Freeserve

The name you type here will be the name of the connection you are creating.

< Back | Next > | Cancel

4

- *[ISP access telephone number]*
- *Next*

This is the number that your modem will dial to connect to your ISP. Don't use spaces.

New Connection Wizard

Phone Number to Dial
What is your ISP's phone number?

Type the phone number below.

Phone number:

08450796699

You might need to include a "1" or the area code, or both. If you are not sure you need the extra numbers, dial the phone number on your telephone. If you hear a modem sound, the number dialed is correct.

< Back | Next > | Cancel

5

⌨ *[user name]*

⌨ *[password]*

⌨ *[confirm password]*

🖱 *Next*

*Enter your user name exactly as agreed with your ISP.
Here you also type in your chosen password, twice.
Note that the password itself is masked on screen so no
snoops peering over your shoulder can see it. Ensure
that the three options are all checked and click Next
again.*

New Connection Wizard

Internet Account Information
You will need an account name and password to sign in to your Internet account.

Type an ISP account name and password, then write down this information and store it in a
safe place. (If you have forgotten an existing account name or password, contact your ISP.)

User name:	macrae34.freeserve.co.uk
Password:	●●●●●●
Confirm password:	●●●●●●

☑ Use this account name and password when anyone connects to the Internet from
this computer

☑ Make this the default Internet connection

☑ Turn on Internet Connection Firewall for this connection

〈 Back   Next 〉   Cancel

6

🖱 *Add a shortcut to this connection to my desktop*

🖱 *Finish*

*Tick the shortcut box and click Finish. That's it – you're
now ready to go online for the first time.*

New Connection Wizard

Completing the New Connection Wizard

You have successfully completed the steps needed to
create the following connection:

Freeserve
* Make this the default connection
* This connection is firewalled
* Share with all users of this computer
* Use the same user name & password for everyone

The connection will be saved in the Network
Connections folder.

☑ Add a shortcut to this connection to my desktop

To create the connection and close this wizard, click Finish.

〈 Back   Finish   Cancel

7

🖱 *Dial*

*As the Wizard closes, you should find that a Connect
window pops up. Click Dial and your modem will
attempt to connect to your ISP. Expect to hear a series
of shrieks from your modem. This is quite normal!*

Connect Freeserve   ？✕

User name:	macrae34.freeserve.co.uk
Password:	*[To change the saved password, click here]*

☑ Save this user name and password for the following users:

○ Me only

◉ Anyone who uses this computer

Dial: 08450796699   ▾

Dial   Cancel   Properties   Help

8

When the modem makes a successful connection to your ISP, an all-important icon appears in the Notification Area on the Taskbar. This is the sign (the only sign, in fact, aside from a temporary balloon) that you are now online.

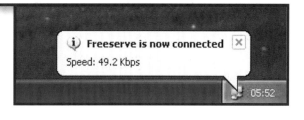

9

ISP Status icon

Disconnect

To disconnect from the internet at any time, double-click this Taskbar icon to launch the Status window. This tells you how long you've been online, your connection speed, and how much data your modem has sent and received. Click the Disconnect button to make your modem 'hang up'. You are now no longer online, and the Taskbar icon disappears.

10

ISP icon

To reconnect, look for the new ISP icon on your Desktop and double-click it. This launches the same window we saw in Step 7. Click the Dial button as before.
Always remember to disconnect *(as in Step 10)* **when you have finished your internet session!**

Browsing the web

OK, so now you can get your computer online with an ISP account. It's time to start exploring the web. We should stress that the web is only one part of the internet but, to be honest, it's the fun part. Once you've mastered a few browser basics, you can visit any web page or website in the world.

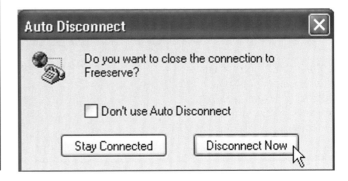

Internet Explorer

A browser is a computer program designed for viewing web pages. Some web pages are little more than a few words of text on a plain background; others are fearsomely interactive, multimedia, full bells-and-whistles affairs. A web*site* is any self-contained but interlinked collection of web pages.

When you type a web page address into a browser, the browser sends a request across the internet to the computer responsible for storing that particular page. If the request is successful, and it usually is, a copy of the page is sent to the browser. That is, the browser *downloads* a copy of the web page onto your computer. What you have to bear in mind here is a simple equation: large web pages take longer to download than small pages because more data has to be transferred across the internet. Large pages tend to have lots of pictures or sounds or animations (or whatever); small pages are mainly text.

Web pages download in fits and starts, with the result that they 'load' in your browser piece by piece. The text may appear first, followed by the images, or vice versa. To see a web page in all its glory, you have to wait for the download to complete.

We're going to work with Internet Explorer in this example, partly because it comes free with Windows and partly because it's overwhelmingly the most popular browser around.

You should find an icon right on your Desktop: double-click this to launch the program. Failing that, there's a link to Internet Explorer on the pinned programs section of the Start Menu (see page 72).

When you double-click the Desktop icon or click its entry in the Start Menu, Internet Explorer generates a Dial-up Connection window (*See above left*). Click Connect and the program will dial

up your ISP. Moreover, if you put a tick in the Connect automatically box, Internet Explorer will in future dial your ISP as soon as it launches without bothering to ask.

If, however, you manually connect to your ISP *before* launching Internet Explorer – as described in the previous section – this window will not appear for the simple reason that the internet connection has already been made. In short, you have a choice: either manually connect to the internet before firing up your browser (or, as we shall see, e-mail program), or let the program do the work.

As soon as Internet Explorer starts, close it again by clicking the red cross in the top right corner of the window. This time, you should see a message similar to the screenshot above right.

Click Disconnect Now and Internet Explorer will automatically disconnect you from your ISP; click Stay Connected and you will stay online even though Internet Explorer itself is no longer running. This would be useful if, for example, you were finished browsing but still had e-mail to check. Alternatively, put a tick in the Don't use Auto Disconnect box and you won't see this message again. You must now remember to close the connection manually every time you wish to end your internet session, as shown in Step 10 on page 127.

If you have a broadband internet service, chances are that none of the above applies, as your internet connection will be 'always on'. However, some ISP software still uses the Dial-up Connection approach so follow the instructions supplied by your service provider.

Browser basics

When you launch Internet Explorer, it should look something like this. Here is a key to all the relevant features.

Menu Bar Click any of the titles here to see a dropdown menu. See page 130 for more details.

Title Bar This displays the title of the web page currently open in the browser. Note the standard minimise window, maximise window and close program buttons at the far right.

Flag This useful icon tells you when Internet Explorer is active and when it's at rest. If the flag is waving, you know that the browser is busy downloading a web page; when it's static, the download is finished and the page should appear complete

in the main window. Your browser may not have a flag icon at all, incidentally: ISPs love to install their own icons here, which is one of the unavoidable consequences of using an ISP-supplied CD-ROM to set up your account.

Toolbar Lots of useful buttons. See page 130 for more details.

Address Bar Action stations! This is where you type the 'address' of a web page in the address box and either press the Enter key or click the Go button at the right end of the Address Bar. Using Enter is usually quicker since your hands are on the keyboard anyway. Every web page has a unique address.

Status Bar Like the flag icon, this tells you about your browser's current activity. The progress bar fills up gradually as a page is downloaded. When it becomes solid green, the page is complete and the bar disappears. More importantly, if you see a yellow padlock, it means the page is *secure* (e.g. on an online shopping website, your credit card details will be safely encrypted).

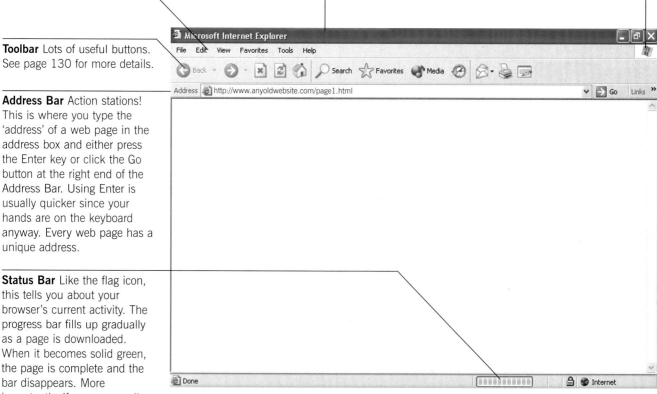

Understanding web addresses

http:// *Hypertext Transfer Protocol, essentially a standard that lets browsers make sense of web pages. You can leave 'http://' out of most web addresses, as Internet Explorer adds it automatically, but only when the next part of the address begins with 'www'.*

www *World Wide Web. The part of the internet concerned with web pages and sites (as opposed to the part concerned with e-mail or newsgroups).*

anyoldwebsite *The domain. This is simply the name of the parent website.*

.com *The suffix. There are lots of these, but '.com' (for company, originally) is the most popular. Country-specific suffixes include '.co.uk' for UK-based companies.*

/ *A forward slash indicates that the next part of the address is a sub-division of the domain, just like a file within a folder.*

page1 *The title of a specific web page. It may have a name, a number or even a bunch of typographical symbols.*

.html *As with the files you create on your computer, web pages have file formats and extensions. HTML – Hypertext Markup Language, with the extension '.html' or '.htm' – is by far the most common language used to design web pages.*

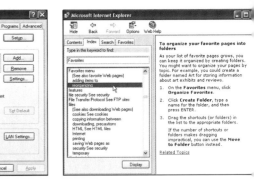

File *Includes the Print Preview function that shows you what a web page will look like on paper before you commit to printing it. You, might, for instance, change the paper layout from portrait to landscape when printing a wide web page (web pages do not have fixed dimensions – they can be as long or as wide as a web designer cares to make them).*

View *If you have difficulty reading tiny text on web pages, use the Text Size command to increase the text from Medium to Larger or Largest. You can also use the Full Screen option to temporarily hide the Toolbars and enlarge a web page to fill the entire screen – a handy feature that reduces the need to scroll.*

Tools *This is where you can configure your browser to the nth degree. In truth, there's little here to worry about, but it is worth checking one setting. Click Tools, then Internet Options, and look in the Connections tab. Your ISP should appear in the main box, and the 'Always dial my default connection' box should be checked. If you were now to select the 'Never dial a connection option', Internet Explorer would stop trying to go online when you launch it. This would be the right choice if you have opted for making manual connections to your ISP, as discussed on page 128.*

Help *Self-evidently, this is where you would seek assistance with your browser. Click Help, then Contents and Index, move to the Index tab, and search for help on any keyword. Try Tip of the Day too, and learn all manner of browser shortcuts. For instance, you can create buttons on a special Links Toolbar for all your favourite web pages.*

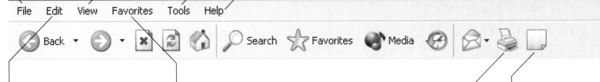

Edit *Includes a useful Find command. Type in a keyword, click Find Next and the word you are looking for will be highlighted on the current web page (if present).*

Favorites *Very important, this one! The Favorites menu is where you store links (called 'bookmarks') to web pages that you wish to return to some other time. There will already be a few entries in your Favorites menu but you can add your own links at will. How? We'll cover that on pages 133-134.*

Print *Click this and the page you're currently viewing will pop straight out of your printer. That's the theory; in practice, web pages have a habit of printing peculiarly so we'd suggest that you use Print Preview first.*

Discuss *Sorry, we've never been able to make this one do anything useful, so we invite you to ignore it completely.*

Back *Surfing is largely a matter of following links – Page A leads to Page B, which takes you to Page C and so forth – and it's very easy to lose track of your starting point. Clicking this button takes you back to the last page you viewed (i.e. click Back while viewing Page C and Page B will reopen).*

Forward. *If, however, you backtrack too far, this button lets you skip forward again, page by page.*

Home *When you launch Internet Explorer, it opens your 'home page'. This might be a Microsoft page, or your ISP's website or any other page. If you tend to visit the same page regularly, why not make this your home page instead? To do this, go online, open the desired web page in your browser, and then do this:*

  Tools

  Internet Options

  General tab

  Use Current

  Apply

  OK

Wherever you are on the web, one click on the Home button will take you straight to this home page.

Favorites *This button displays your bookmarks as clickable links in a special pane on the left side of the browser window – a nice, easy way to work with bookmarks that saves you having to open the Favorites menu every time.*

Search *We're going to ignore this one for now, if you don't mind. We'll explain why on page 135.*

History *Internet Explorer remembers which web pages you visit. Click this button to see them in that left window pane again. You can view the list in different ways and even search for keywords – just experiment with the options at the top of the pane. If, however, you'd prefer your browser to forget your surfing history, perhaps for privacy reasons, do this:*

  Tools

  Internet Options

  General tab

  Clear History

  Yes

  OK

Microsoft Internet Explorer

File Edit View Favorites Tools Help

Back | Search Favorites Media Mail

Stop *Some web pages take forever to appear in your browser, particularly if they are crammed with graphics. Other pages are just '**broken**' and will never download properly, although your browser may not realise this. In either case, press Stop to, er, stop the page in its tracks. Note that you don't have to stop or wait for a page to finish before leaving it for another.*

Refresh *This button forces Internet Explorer to download a web page afresh. This is particularly useful with pages where the content changes regularly – news headlines, for instance, or live sports scores. Every time you press Refresh, you get the most up to date version of the page. It's also worth trying if a page fails to load properly the first time around (e.g. one or more pictures fail to appear or the text is all askance).*

Media *Internet Explorer can play certain kinds of audio and video clips without having to launch a separate program. When you click on a link to such a clip, the browser asks you if that's OK; if you say yes, the clip plays in a special pane to the left of the main window.*

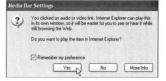

Mail *This button simply fires up your default e-mail program, more of which shortly.*

131

Opening a web page

To open and view a web page, first go online. Now click once in the Address Bar box to position the blinking cursor ready for typing, and type in the address of the page you wish to see. Use lowercase. Press Enter or click the Go button and the page will download and appear in the browser's main window.

DON'T MISS

Enjoy the **Last Night of the Proms** from the comfort of your own computer with

CBBC and **CBeebies**
Blue Peter, Newsround,
Teletubjes, Tweenies...

Learning and
GCSE Bitesize
Holiday Frencl

Entertainment
Comedy, Writers' Room,

Lifestyle
Motoring, Anti

Hyperlinks can be hidden
anywhere on a web page. Uncover
them with the pointer.

If you enter a domain name – something like www.anyoldwebsite.com – the browser will automatically open at the domain's home page, which is usually the best place to start. Otherwise, enter the full address (www.anyoldwebsite.com/page1.html) to go straight to a particular page.

When there is already an address in the box and you want to enter a new one, click on it once. This highlights the entire address. You can either clear it with the Delete key or simply overtype your new address.

Alternatively, position the blinking cursor at the end of the address and clear it with the Backspace key, or at the start and use Delete key. These are the basic skills you practised with WordPad.

If a page is too large for the browser window, scrollbars appear on the right side of the window and perhaps also along the bottom. Use these to navigate through the page. You can also move through a page by rotating the wheel on your mouse, or by using the arrow keys on your keyboard. You can even jump straight to the very top and bottom of a web page by pressing the Home and End keys respectively.

Hyperlinks

A hyperlink is a clickable link on any web page that takes you to any other web page. But how exactly do you recognise them? Well, a hyperlink can be a word, a phrase, an icon, a picture, or *part* of a picture, a box, a button or just about anything at all. The way you tell is by watching the mouse pointer: when it changes shape to a hand with a pointing finger, you've know you've found a hyperlink. Click once, and the browser will open the new page.

An important observation at this juncture. Generally, clicking a hyperlink replaces the current page with a new one. Sometimes, however, clicking a hyperlink opens *another* Internet Explorer window. You now have two Internet Explorers running, each displaying a different web page (*See opposite page*).

You can work with these windows independently – swap between them using the Taskbar buttons – or close either or both at any time. Clicking a hyperlink in either window may well spawn a third window, and so on and so on. It can get confusing but always remember that you can easily resize windows, close them, or minimise them to the Taskbar.

Clicking a link often spawns a fresh browser window.

That old right-click comes in handy on the web.

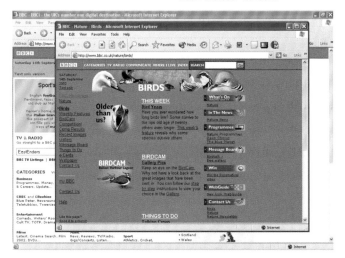

| Open |
| Open in New Window |
| Save Target As |
| Print Target |
| Cut |
| Copy |
| Copy Shortcut |
| Paste |
| Add to Favorites... |
| Properties |

In fact, you can force a hyperlink to open a new window whenever you like. This is particularly useful if you want to use one page as your base: each hyperlink opens a new page in its own window, leaving your original page open and unaffected. To do this, *right*-click a hyperlink and select Open in New Window from the pop-up menu (*See above right*), or hold down the Shift key when you click the link.

The web is vast and chaotic, and you *will* get lost. Indeed, that's part of the fun! Just remember to bookmark good pages as you go along, and use the History function to track down and revisit forgotten pages.

Oh yes, bookmarks …

QUICK Q & A

What's a cookie, and why do web pages keep sending them to my computer?
A cookie is a small text file saved on your computer's hard disk that contains preferences and other information about your use of a website. They are not harmful, and allow a website to, for instance, remember your name next time you visit (assuming that you provide this information in the first place), keep track of your purchases, or just tell how often you visit the site and how long you stay each time. Find out more, including how to stop or delete them, by searching on 'cookie' in Internet Explorer's Help menu.

Bookmarks

To 'bookmark' a web page is to save a link to it on your computer so that you can easily revisit it without ever again having to enter its address in the browser. Here's how.

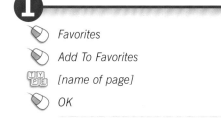

Favorites

Add To Favorites

[name of page]

OK

When you visit a web page that you'd like to return to, add it to the browser's Favorites menu. Click Favorites on the Menu Bar while the page is open, and select Add To Favorites. The Name box shows you the current title of the page but you can change this to something more memorable if you like. Click OK.

2

⊙ *Favorites*

⊙ *[bookmark]*

Click Favorites again and you'll see a list of bookmarks in the dropdown menu. To revisit any bookmarked page, simply select it here and click.

Windows Family Home Page - Microsoft Internet Explorer - [Working O

File Edit View **Favorites** Tools Help

⊙ Back ▾ ⊙ Add to Favorites... ☆ Favorites 🎵 Media

Organize Favorites...

Address http:// Gertrude's Genealogy Resources ▸ 🗎 Clan MacRae

Financial Links ▸ 🗎 Family history

Links ▸ 🗎 Genealogy software

MSN.com 🗎 Online Census

Radio Station Guide

Gertie's Granny's page

3

⊙ *Favorites*

⊙ *Organize Favorites*

⊙ *Create Folder*

⌨ *[name of the folder you wish to create]*

To keep things tidy, you can create your own folders for bookmarks. Return to the Favorites menu, but this time click Organize Favorites. Here you can make new folders and name them to suit. You can also select bookmarks and move them to any specified folder with the Move to Folder button (or, indeed, you can drag-and-drop bookmarks straight to folders).

Organize Favorites   ? ✕

To create a new folder, click on the Create ☆ OldFaves
Folder button. To rename or delete an   🗎 BBC News Front Page
item, select the item and click Rename or   🗎 Yahoo! Mail
Delete.   🗎 BBCi - Weather Centre - 5...
[Create Folder] [Rename]   🗎 Google Glossary
[Move to Folder...] [Delete]   📁 Links
                                               📁 Broadband
New Folder (5)   🗎 AOL.co.uk AOL Broadband
Favorites Folder   🗎 The United Kingdom Pass...
                                               🗎 FSmail - Access your ema...
Modified: 🗎 BAA - GlasgowFlight Arrivals
26/09/2002 16:43

                                               [Close]

4

⊙ *Favorites*

⊙ *Add To Favorites*

⊙ *Create In*

⊙ *[select folder]*

⊙ *OK*

Next time you come to bookmark a page, highlight the relevant folder before clicking OK and the bookmark will be saved within. If there's no suitable folder to hand, you can even make a fresh one at this point by clicking the New Folder button. Remember, you can also work with your bookmarks by clicking the Favorites button on the Toolbar (see page 131).

Add Favorite   ? ✕

☆ Internet Explorer will add this page to your Favorites list. [OK]

   ☐ Make available offline [Customize...] [Cancel]

Name: Online Census   [Create in <<]

Create in: ☆ Favorites   [New Folder...]
               📁 Financial Links
               📁 Gertrude's Genealogy Resources
               📁 Links

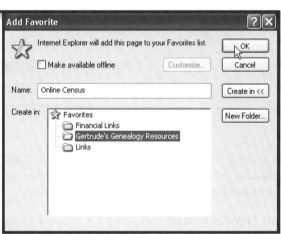

QUICK Q & A

Q: Tell me more about plug-ins.

A: Well, plug-ins, or 'ActiveX components', are free downloadable utilities that super-charge a browser's capabilities. Take Macromedia Flash, for instance. Flash is a coding language sometimes used to design and build entire websites (as an alternative to HTML). Now, if you try to view such a website, you'll be hit with a message that you need the Flash plug-in to proceed. This is unquestionably an irritant, particularly as you are unlikely to know whether or not the site is really worth viewing until you've seen it. The upside, however, is that you only need to download any plug-in once (until the developer releases an upgrade, that is). They generally download reasonably quickly and install semi-automatically.

Searching

To find information on the web, you often have to go looking for it, and this requires the services of a search engine. Search engines are complicated creatures but essentially they roam the web and compile a searchable index of all they find. This index is partial at best – the web is just too vast and in too great a state of flux to ever be pinned down completely – but it's usually sufficient to help you home in on your chosen subject.

There are many search engines around, and you are free to use whichever ones you fancy. Indeed, the reason we glossed over the Internet Explorer's Search button on page 131 is because it links to one particular search engine (operated, unsurprisingly, by a division of Microsoft), and this is rather misleading. We would recommend instead that you experiment with several search engines and bookmark your favourites.

At the time of writing, the most effective search engine *in most cases* is Google. It's also the simplest to use and sports the least fussy interface.

To test drive Google, enter the following web address in your browser's Address Bar – www.google.com – and press Enter or click Go. Now type a keyword or two in the search box, using lowercase, and click the Google Search button.

QUICK Q & A

What other search engines are there?
Oh, plenty. Try Yahoo! (www.yahoo.com), MSN (www.msn.com), AltaVista (www.altavista.com) and Lycos (www.lycos.com) for starters.

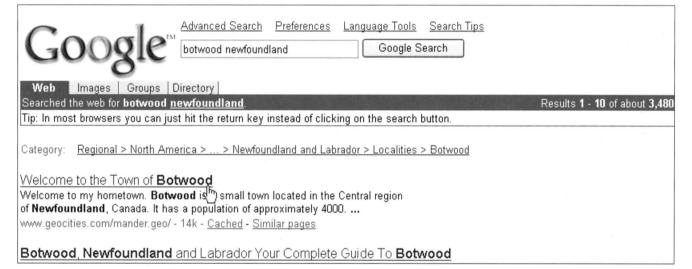

Google then searches through its index and returns a list of web pages that include your keywords.

These are ranked by relevance, which means that the pages at the top of the list are more likely to be what you're looking for than those at the bottom. Each '*hit*' is accompanied with a few lines of text to give the flavour of what the page is all about. Click any blue, underlined page title (i.e. hyperlink) to open that page in your browser.

Google is not infallible, of course – no search engine is – but it does work remarkably well. Two tips: use as many keywords as you can to narrow your searches and increase relevance; and enclose phrases within quotation marks to make Google look for that specific phrase and not just the keywords in any old order.

Downloads

Aside from viewing web pages, you may wish to use your browser to download files: an application form, perhaps, or a plug-in, or a video clip or sound file, or even a program. Downloading a file involves transferring a copy of it from some computer somewhere to your own computer's hard disk.

Let's try it out. For our example, we'll download a free music player called Winamp. This program may not be available forever, and the web pages we work with here may change appearance. However, the purpose of this example is to illustrate a fairly standard download procedure.

Internet Explorer icon

www.winamp.com [Enter]

[link]

Launch your browser and enter the web page address quoted above. The trick now is to find the hyperlink that leads to the download page. Winamp actually makes this easy – just click the big obvious picture – but sometimes you have to root around to find the right link.

Begin download

There are several versions of Winamp available but here we want the full version. It's over 3 Megabytes in size so this will take around 8–10 minutes to download with a modem. Click the link to proceed.

Get Winamp3

Only Winamp3 Full is available right now - Winamp3 Standard and Winamp3 Lite are coming soon. Click the "Begin Download" button to start downloading. Click here if you have a Macintosh!

Features	Lite	Standard	Full
MP3 Audio Support	✓	✓	✓
SHOUTcast Radio Support	✓	✓	✓
Skins and Components Support	✓	✓	✓
Winamp Visualization Studio		✓	✓
Windows Media Audio Support			✓
Built In Ads	NONE	NONE	NONE
Cost	FREE!	FREE!	FREE!
File Size to Download	? KB	? MB	3.18 MB
Choose a Version	Getting warm...	Getting warmer...	⊙ Full

Begin Download!
click here

Save

Up pops a File Download window. Internet Explorer is asking what you want to do with the target file (i.e. the Winamp program). You want to save it to your hard disk, so click the Save button.

File Download

? You are downloading the file:

winamp3_0-full.exe from download.nullsoft.com

Would you like to open the file or save it to your computer?

[Open] [Save] [Cancel] [More Info]

☑ Always ask before opening this type of file

④

🖰 *Desktop*

🖰 *Save*

Now you have to tell the browser where to save the file. We recommend that you use the Desktop – it's easy to find the file when the download is complete – so select Desktop from the dropdown Save in: box and click Save.

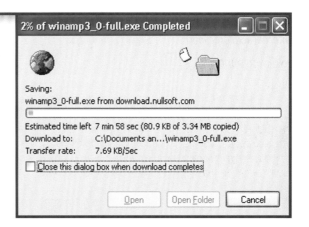

⑤

Make a cup of tea

Well, you can monitor the process of the download if you like, or you can go and do something more interesting. In any case, let Internet Explorer complete the download before you start any fresh work on your computer.

⑥

🖰 *Close*

🖰🖰 *winamp icon*

When the download completes, click Close. Now close down Internet Explorer and come offline. On the Desktop you will find an icon representing the newly downloaded file. Double-click this now to launch the program installation.

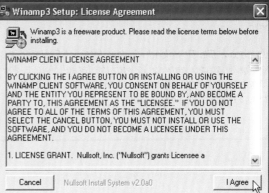

⑦

🖰 *I Agree*

🖰 *Next*

🖰 *Install*

The rest is basically a case of following instructions. Installation procedures vary considerably so skip back to page 102 for an overview. However, the key thing here is that you've found a useful, free program on the internet and downloaded it to your computer. Well done!

E-mail

Away from the wonders of web pages, we find the internet's true 'killer application' – e-mail. Those of us who have been using e-mail for years now take it so much for granted that even a temporary blip in the service can induce panic ('I can't live without my Inbox!'); those who come to it anew are soon swayed by e-mail's immediacy and, dare we say it, simplicity.

There are free web-based e-mail services available, like Hotmail, so it is in fact possible to send and receive messages using only Internet Explorer. However, we're going to use the specialist e-mail software that comes with Windows – Outlook Express – and take advantage of the type of e-mail service typically provided by ISPs.

How does e-mail work (roughly)?

'Will I still get my messages if I'm not online when they arrive?'
'Will I still get my messages when the computer's turned off?'
'Will I still get my messages if I go on holiday?'
Yes, yes, and three times yes. To understand how e-mail works, it helps to picture a whole bunch of 'mail *servers*' connected together in the internet. A mail server is a computer responsible for storing and forwarding e-mail messages on yours and everybody else's behalf.

Let's suppose that Jack sends you an e-mail, and that your e-mail address is angus.fridge@groovyisp.com. His computer's modem sends the message through the telephone line to his ISP, where it is received by a mail server. This computer then checks the latter part of the delivery address – the bit after the @ sign – and sends the message off to another mail server somewhere on the internet en route to your ISP. Now, the message may take a convoluted and, indeed, global route, passing through many different mail servers in many geographical locations, but eventually it winds up on a mail server owned by Groovy ISP. This computer then identifies the ultimate recipient (i.e. you) from the first part of the e-mail address, and sticks it in a holding area, a little like a pigeon hole. Next time you log on to the internet and look for new messages, the server sends Jack's e-mail to your computer. If you don't check your e-mail for days at a time, that's just fine.

A couple of quick notes. Any ISP will only hold uncollected e-mail for a certain specified period – normally a few weeks, sometimes months – so don't leave it too long. Also, ISPs usually impose a size limit on e-mails, typically five or ten megabytes per message. This is understandable, as mail servers would soon fill up if required to store hundreds of Gigabytes of uncollected mail indefinitely. Furthermore, large e-mails take longer to send and receive because more data has to be transferred across the internet. You should always remember that the recipient of your messages probably has to pay telephone charges while connected to the internet, and nobody will thank you for an unasked-for 'funny' video clip that takes twenty minutes to download.

Configuring Outlook Express

Let's set up Outlook Express as your e-mail program. (Again, if you used a CD-ROM supplied by your ISP to set up your account, all of this may be pre-configured.) When you run the program for the very first time, the Internet Connection Wizard may pop right up, in which case skip to Step 2.

1

Start

E-mail icon

Outlook Express

Set up a Mail account

There is a shortcut to Outlook Express in the pinned programs part of the Start Menu. When the program launches, click Outlook Express in the upper of the two panes on the left side. In the main window, look for an option to set up a Mail account. Click this now to launch the Internet Connection Wizard.

2

[your name]

Next

When somebody receives an e-mail from you, this is how you will be identified. Type in your name exactly as you wish it to appear.

3

[your e-mail address]

Next

This is the e-mail address arranged with your ISP when you first signed up. Be sure to enter it accurately. E-mail addresses are always lowercase.

4

[incoming mail server]

[outgoing mail server]

🖱 *Next*

The tricky bit. Here you must enter the names of your ISP's mail servers. You can only get this information from your ISP but it would have been provided when you signed up. If not, give them a call.

Internet Connection Wizard

E-mail Server Names

My incoming mail server is a [POP3 ▾] server.

Incoming mail (POP3, IMAP or HTTP) server:
[pop.freeserve.net]

An SMTP server is the server that is used for your outgoing e-mail.

Outgoing mail (SMTP) server:
[smtp.freeserve.net]

[< Back] [Next >] [Cancel]

5

[account name]

[password]

🖱 *Next*

🖱 *Finish*

Now fill in your account name and password. These are just the user name and password you used in Step 6 on page 126. Check the Remember password box and you won't have to enter it again. Click Next and then Finish in the final window. Your e-mail program is now ready to use.

Internet Connection Wizard

Internet Mail Logon

Type the account name and password your Internet service provider has given you.

Account name: [macrae34.freeserve.co.uk]

Password: [••••••]
☑ Remember password

If your Internet service provider requires you to use Secure Password Authentication (SPA) to access your mail account, select the 'Log On Using Secure Password Authentication (SPA)' check box.

☐ Log on using Secure Password Authentication (SPA)

[< Back] [Next >] [Cancel]

? QUICK Q & A

Somebody asked me to stop sending 'rich text' messages. What's that all about, then?
In the context of Outlook Express, rich text is essentially the same language as that used to design web pages (i.e. HTML). This lets you tweak font size and colour, insert pictures right into the body of a message, add fancy backgrounds, and so forth. However, all such padding adds to the size of a message, so rich text e-mails are slower to send and receive. Moreover, not all e-mail programs can read rich text messages properly, so your words of wit and wisdom may not be reaching their target intact. You can easily configure Outlook Express to generate only unformatted messages thus:

🖱 Tools

🖱 Options

🖱 Send tab

🖱 Plain Text

E-mail basics

When you launch Outlook Express, it should look something like this. Here is a key to all the relevant features.

Title Bar *This shows you which folder is currently open within the program. Note the standard minimise window, maximise window and close program buttons at the far right.*

Folders pane *Outlook Express lets you work with e-mail messages in a series of folders. Here we find:*

Inbox *Incoming messages are stored here.*

Outbox *A holding area for messages ready to be sent the next time the computer connects to the internet.*

Sent Items *Once a message has been sent, it moves from the Outbox folder to Sent Items. This gives you a record of your outgoing messages.*

Deleted Items *Much like the Windows Recycle Bin (see page 68), this folder is a holding area for messages that you have deleted. You can permanently delete messages from here by right-clicking the Deleted Items icon and selecting Empty 'Deleted Items' Folder from the pop-up menu.*

Drafts *If you save a message midway through composition, this is where it is kept. You can retrieve a draft message at any time to continue working on it.*

Contacts pane *You can store contact details here to save having to remember people's e-mail addresses. Click the arrow next to the word Contacts, then New Contact, and complete a 'card' for each contact. By default, Outlook Express automatically creates a contact card every time you reply to a message from a new correspondent. To delete a contact, highlight the entry in the Contacts pane and press the Delete key.*

Toolbar *Nice big buttons that do obvious things. We'll look at these in turn when we practise working hands-on with Outlook Express.*

Menu Bar *As with Internet Explorer, click any word for a dropdown menu. The most useful of these is the Options section of the Tools menu. Here you can, for example, configure Outlook Express to automatically check for new messages every so many minutes while you're online.*

Message pane *This is where you view pertinent details about messages stored in any of the folders in the Folder pane – the 'subject' of the message, and who sent it, and when. Again, we'll see this in action shortly.*

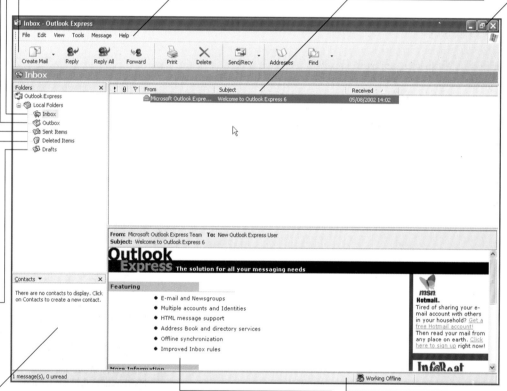

Preview pane *In this window, you can read the message selected in the Message pane above. Note the scrollbar on the right for scrolling through long messages. Here we see the standard welcome message that accompanies Outlook Express (it's worth a read).*

Status bar *This tells you a little about the program's current activity.*

Sending and receiving e-mail

We will now send and receive an e-mail message. But before we start, a word about using Outlook Express on- and offline.

If your computer is already connected to the internet when you launch Outlook Express, you can check for new messages very easily by clicking the Send/Recv button on the Toolbar. You can also compose a message and send it immediately. However, if your computer is not currently connected, Outlook Express will ask whether you wish to go online now (*see below*).

The correct response rather depends upon your intentions. If you wish to check for new messages and perhaps scribble a quick reply or two, we'd suggest going online straight away. Click Yes and Outlook Express will dial up your ISP and make the connection.

If, on the other hand, you wish to compose a lengthy new e-mail, click No. Now you can work on your message at your leisure, perhaps even saving it in the Draft folder and completing it later, without having to pay telephone charges all the while.

In this example, we will begin in offline mode, so take it as read that we clicked the No button.

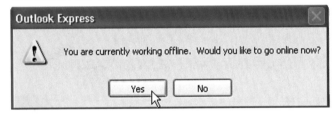

?

QUICK Q & A

How do I know that my e-mail message has been delivered?
In fact, you don't – but you will find out if it hasn't been delivered. Any message that fails to reach its destination is 'bounced' back to you by a mail server and re-appears in your Inbox with a note to that effect. By far the most common reason for non-delivery is getting somebody's e-mail address slightly wrong. There is no margin for error here. This is why it helps to use Contacts and the Address Book in Outlook Express, as you only ever have to type the address correctly once (and not even that if you reply to a message from a contact; remember, Outlook Express automatically creates contact details for your correspondents).

1

 Create Mail

[e-mail address]

Click the Create Mail button on the Toolbar. Up pops an e-mail window. Remember, you can easily resize this window (see page 32). The blinking cursor is already in the To: box, so type your correspondent's e-mail address here. In this case, we'd suggest that you send your first e-mail to ... yourself.

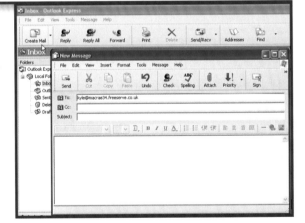

2

[subject line]

All e-mail messages have a short subject line, which might be a simple 'Hello' or a potted summary of the message, like 'Here's that business report you asked for.' Click once in the Subject: box to move the blinking cursor, and then start typing.

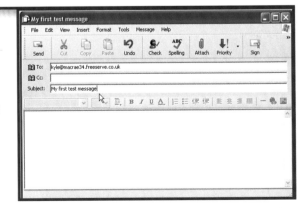

3

 [message]

🖰 Send

Now click anywhere within the main message window to move the blinking cursor into that area, and type the 'body' of your message. This is just like using WordPad (see pages 40-47). When you're finished, click the Send button on the e-mail window's Toolbar (not, note, the main program Toolbar).

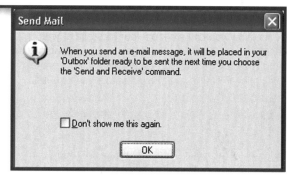

4

🖰 OK

At this point, the e-mail window disappears and Outlook Express informs you that your message will be transferred to the Outbox. Click OK. If you had been online at this point, the message would be sent immediately.

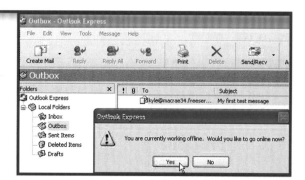

5

🖰 Send/Recv

🖰 Yes

Click the Send/Recv button on the main program Toolbar and confirm that you wish to go online. Outlook Express now dials up your ISP and sends the message. At the same time, the program also checks for any new messages for you on your ISP's incoming mail server. If so, it retrieves them and files them in your Inbox folder.

6

🖰 Send/Recv

🖰 Inbox

🖰 [select message]

In this case, we fully expect delivery of our test message. Wait a minute or so and click Send/Recv again. When you see a blue figure appear next to the Inbox folder in the Folders pane – this is the number of unread messages awaiting your attention – click Inbox. Now select the test message by clicking the little closed envelope icon next to the sender's name. The body of the message will be displayed in the Preview pane.

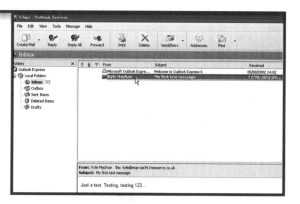

- [select message]
- Reply
- [message]
- Send

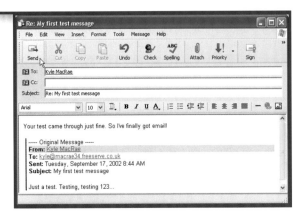

Let's now reply to this message. Select the message in the Message pane as before and click the Reply button on the main Toolbar. This opens a new e-mail window in which the recipient's name already appears in the To: box (this is actually an e-mail address in disguise). What's more, the message to which you are replying is automatically 'quoted' within the body of this new message. This helps correspondents keep track of an e-mail conversation. The blinking cursor will be blinking invitingly in the message window at this point, so type your reply message and click Send. This time, because you are already online, the message departs almost immediately (it moves to the Outbox for a few seconds first).

- Send/Recv
- Inbox
- [select message]

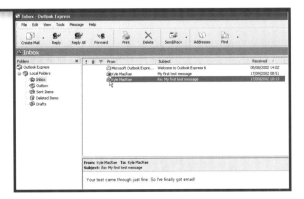

Once more, click the Send/Recv button to check for new messages, then select this latest e-mail when it arrives in the Inbox. Note that the subject line is now prefixed by 'Re:'. This is Outlook Express's way of flagging that a message is a reply to another message. You have now sent yourself an e-mail, replied to it, and received the reply. Sending and receiving e-mail to a wider audience works in exactly the same way.
When you close Outlook Express, you should see the same Auto Disconnect box that popped up when closing Internet Explorer (see page 128).

Getting fancy

We have really only scratched the surface of e-mail's possibilities, so here are a few suggestions that you may care to play with.

1

Deleting. *To delete a message, select it in the Message pane and either press the* *key or drag it to the Deleted Items folder.*

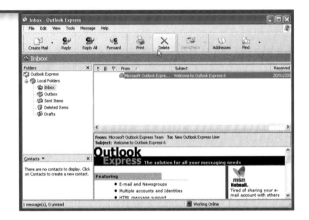

2

Forwarding. *You can forward a copy of any received message to any correspondent. Select the message in the Message pane, click the Forward button on the Toolbar, and enter the recipient's e-mail address. You can add your own comments in the message window or click Send now to forward the message just as it arrived.*

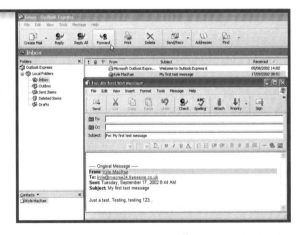

3

Contacts. *When composing an e-mail message, click the little icon next to the To: button. This fires up the Address Book – a list of all your existing contacts. Highlight the relevant name, click the To: button and then click OK. This automatically enters the recipient's e-mail address in the e-mail window.*

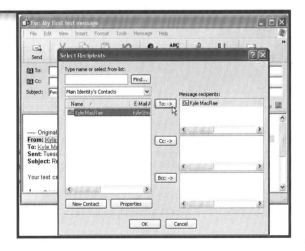

4

Carbon copy. *If you want to send the same e-mail to two people simultaneously, enter the second e-mail address in the Cc: box. If you want to send it to multiple recipients, separate each address with a semi-colon.*

5

Spelling. *Outlook Express can check your spelling when you compose a message. Click Tools followed by Options and then Spelling, and check the 'Always check spelling' box.*

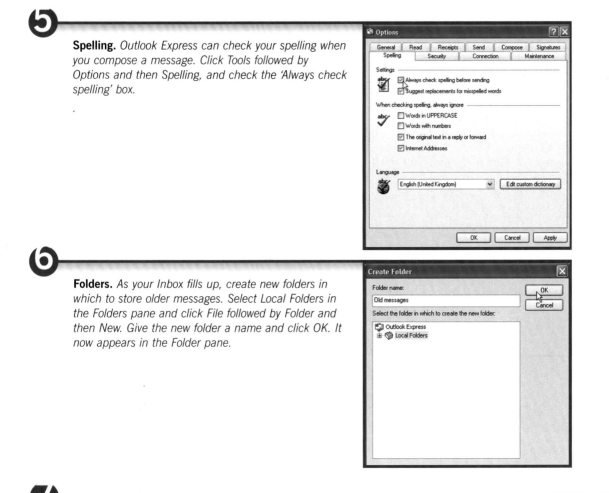

6

Folders. *As your Inbox fills up, create new folders in which to store older messages. Select Local Folders in the Folders pane and click File followed by Folder and then New. Give the new folder a name and click OK. It now appears in the Folder pane.*

7

File messages. *To file an e-mail, select it in the Message pane and drag-and-drop it on the target folder in the Folder pane. The message now moves from the Inbox to that folder. Alternatively, right-click the message, select Move to Folder from the pop-up menu, and select the target folder from the list.*

8

Attaching files. *You can send a copy of a file from your computer's hard disk to an e-mail correspondent. Compose a message as usual then click the Attach button in the e-mail window. Find the file on your computer, and click Attach. Remember, your ISP will impose limits on the size of files that can be e-mailed. As a guide, 500 **Kilobytes** (half of one Megabyte) is about as big as you should go unless both you and the recipient have a broadband connection and you have asked permission to send a large file.*

9

Viewing an attachment. *Likewise, people can send you files with e-mail. You know when you've received an attachment because (a) the message takes longer to download, and (b) a paperclip icon appears next to the message in the Message pane.*
To save the attachment, click the larger paperclip icon at the top of the Preview pane, select Save Attachments from the menu, and pick a suitable folder on your hard disk. As always, we'd suggest the My Documents folder or a sub-folder within it.
And what of viruses? Quite right. See page 148.

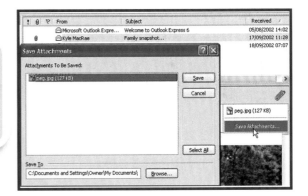

?

QUICK Q & A

How can I check how big a file is before I e-mail it?
You can check the size of any file by navigating to it with My Documents, right-clicking its icon, and selecting Properties from the pop-up menu. Its size will be expressed in bytes if it's tiny, Kilobytes if it's bigger, and Megabytes if it's a whopper.

10

Inserting pictures. *You can even place a picture file right into the body of an e-mail message. To do this, compose your message as usual and click Insert on the e-mail window Toolbar. Now click Picture and then use the Browse button to locate the image on your hard disk. Click Open and OK and the picture will appear in the body of the message, below any text you have typed.*

Internet nasties

Sadly, the internet has a downside, and it's considerable.
Here we touch upon a few net-borne nasties.

Viruses, and how to avoid them

Broadly speaking, a computer virus is a small software program
with the potential to do damage to your computer's settings, to
delete or modify your files, to allow a third party to access your
hard disk without your knowledge, to replicate itself and spread
from computer to computer, to do nothing of any consequence
whatsoever, or any combination of the above. They go by the
name of worms, script viruses, macro viruses, Trojan horses and
more. They are all to be avoided.

Most viruses these days are delivered and spread by e-mail,
usually in the form of a file attachment. Opening the attachment
launches the virus, at which point your computer is infected and
the damage is done. A particularly virulent virus can then e-mail
itself to everybody in your contacts list, thereby spreading
exponentially and globally.

However – and we really cannot stress this strongly enough –
you can avoid viruses by taking a few simple precautions.

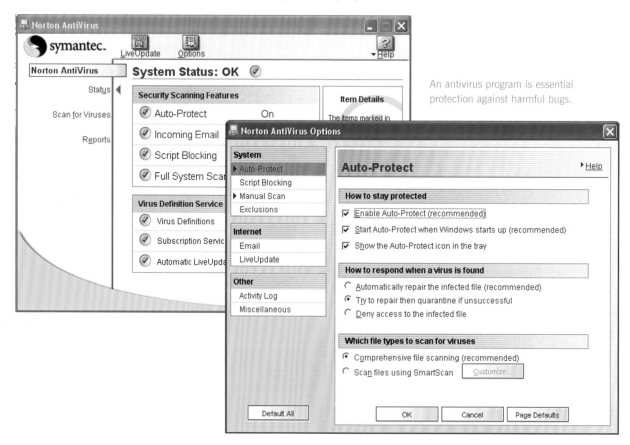

An antivirus program is essential
protection against harmful bugs.

First and foremost, buy and install some antivirus software. Then read the manual carefully and configure the program to work at the maximum protection level. This ensures that, among other things, it automatically 'scans' e-mail attachments for viruses.

It is equally important to download regular updates from the developer's website to ensure that you're always protected against recently discovered viruses. Just about every antivirus program worth the purchase price can be easily configured to update itself automatically.

Furthermore, *never* open an e-mail attachment unless you know the sender and you are expecting the file. True, your antivirus software should detect the virus but it's always possible for a brand new virus or a previously unseen mutation to slip through the net.

For maximum safety, do away with the Preview pane in Outlook Express. Merely viewing a message can, on occasion, lead to infection. To do this, click View on the Toolbar, then Layout, and uncheck the Show Preview pane box. Now click Apply and OK.

In practice, virus hoaxes are almost as damaging as the real thing. Mark these words, one day you'll receive an e-mail that (a) graphically describes a new 'undetectable' virus that will allegedly chew up your hard disk and spit it out, and (b) exhort you to warn everybody you know without delay. Sheer nonsense, of course, but people are fooled every time. Whenever you see such a message, check it out before acting. An excellent website that sorts hoaxes from the real thing is Vmyths: www.vmyths.com.

Firewalls, and how to use them

A firewall is a software barrier that stops somebody from accessing your PC through the internet – and perhaps stealing or deleting your files –without your say-so. There are many commercial firewalls around but Windows XP also has its own firewall built in.

Pop-ups, and how to kill them

The world wide web is riddled with intrusive advertising. Indeed, on many websites, it's hard to find the real content amidst all the banner ads and eye-catching 'special offers'. What really drives us mad, though, are pop-ups – that is, adverts that appear in a separate window without so much as a by-your-leave. There you are, happily reading a web page, when up pops an advert for, say, a credit card. Your view is obscured and you have to close this unasked-for window before you can proceed. Some pop-ups are more persistent and just keep popping up time after time.

Worse, many adverts are disguised as computer error messages or warnings, and it's all too easy to think that Windows is trying to tell you something. It's not – somebody is trying to sell you something. Some ads even have what looks like a Close button, but this is just another trick: click the fake 'button' and you'll be taken straight to the advertiser's website.

Our advice is keep your wits about you as you surf. Close pop-ups as soon as they appear, and avoid clicking any advert unless you genuinely do want to find out more. If pop-ups become a plague, consider getting a software utility that stops them in their tracks. One such is called Pop-Up Stopper. It can be downloaded free of charge from Panicware at www.panicware.com.

Live without the Preview Pane for increased security.

Keep hackers at bay with a firewall.

A pop-up ad pretending to be something useful. Get wise to such nonsense.

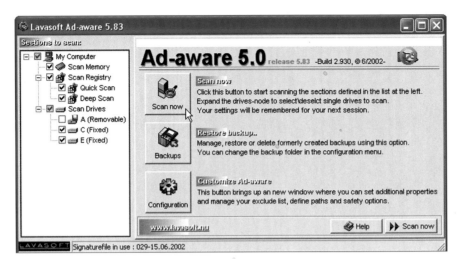

Rid your system of sneaky spyware with this free utility.

Spyware, and how to sniff it out

Even worse than pop-ups are programs that worm their way into your computer, surreptitiously monitor your surfing, and report back to base. These 'spyware' programs usually masquerade as some really helpful utility, but you should never, ever install anything unless you're absolutely sure that you need and want it.

Spyware should not be confused with plug-ins, however. A plug-in is a browser enhancement that lets you view special web pages and certain multimedia effects. These are usually worth downloading and installing – in fact, the likes of Macromedia Flash Player or Apple QuickTime are essential to view some websites at all. Again, be careful and selective. Two free anti-spyware programs that we use and like are Ad-aware, from LavaSoft (**www.lavasoftusa.com**), and Windows Defender from Microsoft (**http://www.microsoft.com/athome/security/spyware/software/default.mspx**).

Spam, and how to live with it

Spam is unsolicited commercial e-mail, the electronic equivalent of junk mail but with one important difference: it's you who pays for it (in terms of telephone charges for your internet connection). Spam is a huge pain in the posterior.

However, you can destroy spam as quickly as it arrives in your Inbox with a single press of the Delete key. You can also, if you wish, report offending e-mails to SpamCop at http://spamcop.net (this, incidentally, is an example of a web address where you do need to include the 'http://' partly because there is no 'www' prefix. What you must never do – never, ever, ever – is reply to a spam message, especially if it has a 'click here to unsubscribe from our mailing list' option. This merely confirms that your e-mail address is 'live', and you'll be inundated with fresh spam before you can say 'delicious pork luncheon meat has no connection with unsolicited commercial bulk e-mail whatsoever.'

You can also limit the flow by keeping your e-mail address as private as possible. That is, don't use it in public *web forums* or *newsgroups* – spammers 'harvest' addresses wherever they can find them – and don't register for any product or service on the internet unless you're happy that the company won't sell, rent or otherwise disseminate your personal data for marketing purposes. Best of all, keep one e-mail address as a deliberate spam magnet, and use it in place of your primary, personal address whenever there's a risk of attracting spam. A web-based e-mail service is perfect for this.

Using the Windows Security Center

Sorry about the spelling of 'center' – even though our computer is set to use UK English, Microsoft insists on using American spellings for some Windows features. Security Center is one of them, and it's an essential part of Windows: it makes sure your PC has the most up-to-date version of Windows together with any security patches and bug fixes, and it can also protect you from online nasties who try to connect to your PC over the internet. Here's how it works.

To run Security Center, open Control Panel and look for the very last option. Double-click it and you should see a screen like this one, with traffic light-style pictures giving you a quick summary of how secure your PC is. The three green lights you see here mean we're well protected. Click the Windows Firewall link at the bottom to see the firewall settings in more detail.

Windows Firewall prevents unauthorised users from accessing your PC over the internet, and it should be switched on unless you've bought another firewall program. Firewall normally lets some programs connect to the internet – such as music software or the ActiveSync software for Pocket PCs – but if you're using a public internet connection such as an airport wireless network, it's a good idea to tick 'Don't Allow Exceptions' for maximum security.

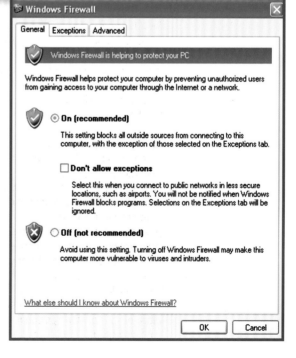

3

If you'd like to see what Windows features or programs are allowed to accept incoming internet connections, click the Exceptions tab. If there's a program in the list that looks dodgy, you can remove it from the Exceptions list by clicking on it and then clicking Delete.

4

For maximum protection, your copy of Security Center should look like this: green lights for Firewall, for Automatic Updates and for Virus Protection. Windows XP doesn't come with its own virus protection, but there are lots of options from firms such as McAfee (**www.mcafee.com**) and Symantec (**www.symantec.com**).

5

It's a very good idea to visit Microsoft Update to get the latest patches and security updates for Windows. To do this, open Internet Explorer and click Help followed by Windows Update. To see a full list of available options, click the Custom button.

6

The available updates are broken into three categories: High Priority, which you should install immediately; Software, Optional, which update programs you have on your PC; and Hardware, Optional, which provides updates to help your PC hardware work more smoothly. To view the updates in each category, click the links in the left-hand column.

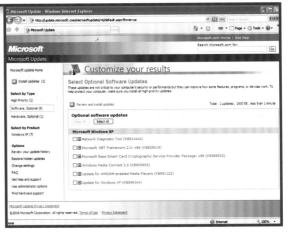

7

In this screenshot we've clicked Hardware, Optional in the left-hand side of the Microsoft Update screen. There's an update available for our printer software, so we'll add that to our download list. To do this, just click the box next to the update. A tick should appear in the box.

8

When you've chosen the updates you want to install, click Review And Install Updates. You should now see a screen like the one shown here, with a list of your chosen updates together with any compulsory updates such as fixes for Windows XP. Click Install Updates to start the installation process.

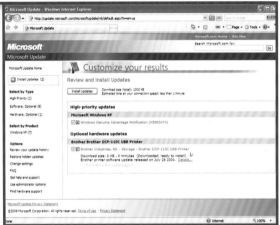

9

When you click the Install Updates button you'll usually have to agree to the download's licence agreement – and if you're downloading lots of different updates, then you may have to agree to a separate licence for each. It's annoying, but once you've got past the legalese you'll see the progress bar shown here as your updates are downloaded and installed.

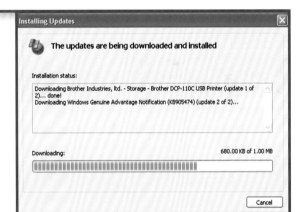

10

Don't worry if you see an error message like this one – it doesn't mean that there's a problem. While most of the updates you download via Microsoft Update install immediately, in some cases you'll need to restart your PC in order to complete the installation process. That's what we've got here: in order to update our printer software, we'll need to restart.

PART 5

Appendices

Appendix 1
System Restore

On day one, your brand new computer will 'just work'. But on day two, and day three, and forever thereafter, you run the risk of trouble. One day, inevitably, your computer either won't start at all or will start misbehaving – and come that day, you'll wish that you could roll back time and undo whatever it was that caused the trouble.

Well, you can, thanks to System Restore – a rescue routine for your computer.

Good practice

System Restore works by taking regular 'snapshots' (called restore points) of your computer's most important settings. Should something go awry, you have the opportunity to revert to an earlier restore point and, hopefully, recover from the problem.

System Restore works in the background and really needs very little thought or intervention. It creates restore points automatically whenever you install a Windows Update (p.152) or install a new program. However, it doesn't hurt to occasionally make restore points manually, particularly just before (not after!) making any significant change to your computer, such as plugging in a new piece of hardware. Also, because Windows doesn't *always* recognise new program installations, we'd strongly recommend that you make a manual restore point before loading any new software. Here's how …

Making and restoring a restore point

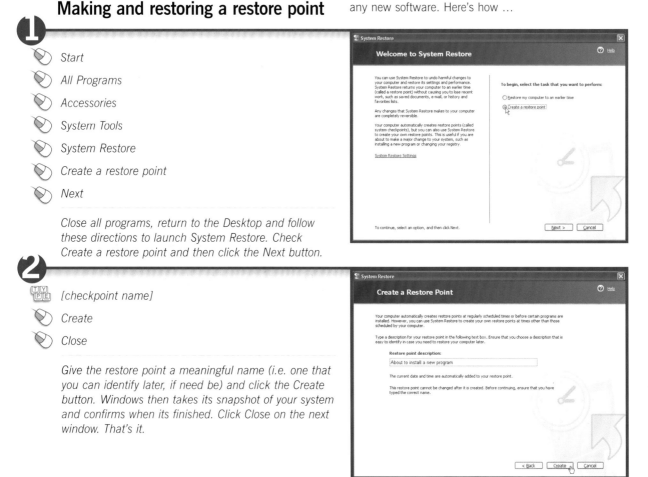

① *Start*

All Programs

Accessories

System Tools

System Restore

Create a restore point

Next

Close all programs, return to the Desktop and follow these directions to launch System Restore. Check Create a restore point and then click the Next button.

② *[checkpoint name]*

Create

Close

Give the restore point a meaningful name (i.e. one that you can identify later, if need be) and click the Create button. Windows then takes its snapshot of your system and confirms when its finished. Click Close on the next window. That's it.

3

- *Start*
- *All Programs*
- *Accessories*
- *System Tools*
- *System Restore*
- *Restore my computer to an earlier time*

- *Next*
- *Select restore point*
- *Next*

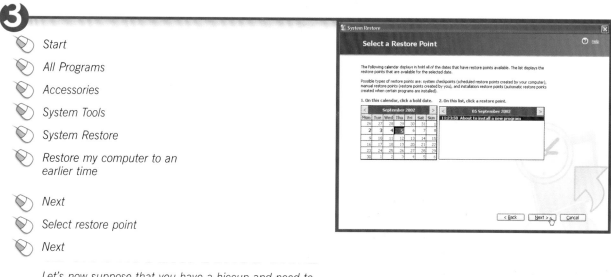

Let's now suppose that you have a hiccup and need to revert to your last restore point.
Launch System Restore as above but this time select the Restore option. In the next window, a calendar appears, and you can click on any day to see a list of possible restore points. However, the computer's most recent point is displayed by default – in this case, the one we just made. Select it and click Next.

4

- *Next*
- *OK*

The next window is your last chance to opt out of the process; click the Next button and Windows shuts down, restores the system to the way it was when you made the selected restore point, and restarts. Click OK when you see the confirmation window.

Life saver

Now, if this solves the problem with your computer, great. Otherwise, you can either undo the restoration – you'll see an option to do just that if you run System Restore again – or restore your computer to an even earlier time.

Incidentally, System Restore works entirely at a deep-rooted level and does not affect your own files and folders, so don't worry that you'll lose today's work if you roll back to yesterday's restore point.

In rare circumstances, Windows may be unable to start your computer normally. Should this happen, System Restore will kick in before Windows starts. Pick the most recent restore point and see if that gets Windows working; otherwise, keep trying earlier points.

PART **5**

Appendix 2
Eight of the best

In addition to the must-have security programs that protect your PC, there's stacks of software that can make your PC a nicer place – and save you a great deal of time, effort and in some cases, cash. Whether you want to use your computer as a digital jukebox, find things fast or simply chat with your friends, the following programs will make your PC smarter, smoother and more fun. Over the next few pages we'll describe the ten programs we think every PC owner should download. We love them all, and we think you'll love them too – and not just because every single one of them is free.

Firefox
www.mozilla.com/firefox

Every PC comes with Microsoft's web browser, Internet Explorer, but we think Firefox is better. It's fast, easy to use and in many cases safer than Microsoft's browser, and you can change the way it looks by downloading free Themes or add new features by downloading free Extensions. For example the list of available extensions includes advert-blocking, download managers, tools that help you find interesting sites, and even tools that display the football results. We've been using Firefox for a few years now, and while the latest version of Internet Explorer is a vast improvement on its predecessor we think Firefox still has the edge.

Copernic Desktop Search
www.copernic.com

The more you use your PC, the harder it becomes to find things: for example, in our e-mail program we have 210 online shopping receipts, 71 different usernames and passwords for websites, 3,845 personal e-mails, 12,243 work e-mails … and that's just from the last two years. Add in 4,026 word documents, more than 1,000 text files, 300 PDF documents, 8,642 digital photos and 4,862 MP3 music files and finding anything is like looking for a very small needle in a very large haystack. Hurrah, then, for Copernic: this free download keeps an eye on your files and searches through e-mails, files, music, photos, contacts and even your web browsing history to find what you want – fast.

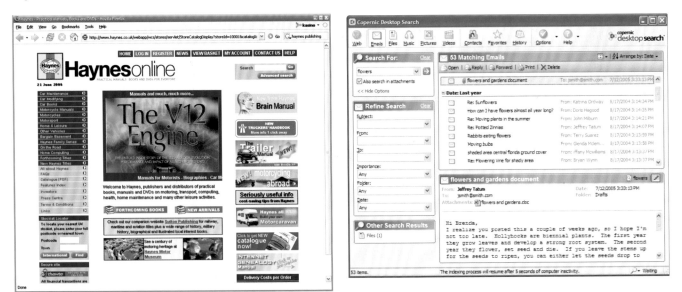

Skype

www.skype.com

For a little program, Skype has got a lot of big companies worried. When you install Skype on your PC you can make phone calls to other Skype users for free, no matter where they are in the world. Thanks to an additional, low-cost service called SkypeOut, you can even call people's landlines and mobile phones from your PC. Telephone companies are terrified of Skype and its rivals (for example, at the time of writing it's possible to run Skype on a Windows-powered mobile phone) because it slashes the cost of calling to zero for Skype to Skype calls and it makes international calling charges look very steep indeed. If you think it's good to talk, Skype will save you a fortune.

Yahoo! Widgets

http://widgets.yahoo.com

Yahoo! Widgets won't save you money or make your PC run more smoothly, but it's a lot of fun. Widgets are little programs that appear on your desktop. The range includes little boxes that show the weather forecast, wireless network signal strength or your PC's performance. You can also install Widget tools including calculators, to-do lists, calendars and much, much more. You can even run a Werewolf Monitor, which shows you the current phase of the moon in case you 'need to make sure you're locked away when the next full moon comes around'.

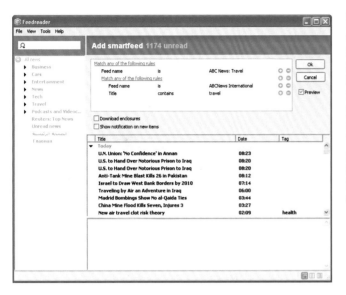

FeedReader
www.feedreader.com

FeedReader enables you to subscribe to your favourite websites using a technology called RSS, which stands for 'Really Simple Syndication'. Most big-name sites (and most blogs) publish RSS feeds. If you use FeedReader you can read the feeds in a program that looks a bit like your e-mail software. One of the big advantages of a feed reading program is that you can create 'smart feeds', which combine several different feeds into a kind of personalised newspaper – so for example if you're interested in computers you could create a smart feed that combines stories from *The Guardian's* technology section, from The Register news site and from a few blogs.

The Google Pack
http://pack.google.com

Google isn't just a search engine: it offers lots of PC software too, and the Google Pack is a superb collection of utilities. You get Picasa, which makes it easy to organise and edit your digital photos; Google Desktop, which is a bit like the Copernic Desktop Search; Google Earth, which you can use to explore satellite photos and up-to-date maps of the entire planet, and a range of programs including security software and a video player.

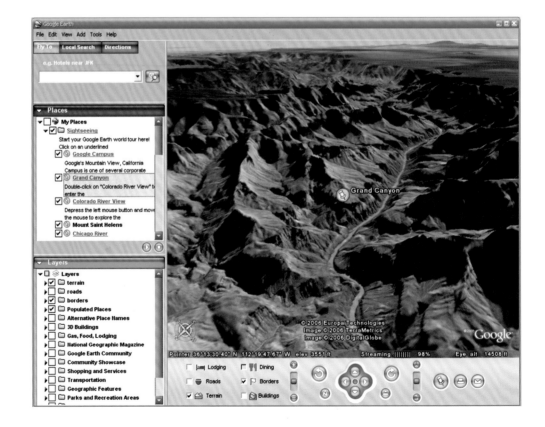

Windows XP Power Toys

www.microsoft.com/windowsxp/downloads/powertoys/
xppowertoys.mspx

Power Toys are little programs that Microsoft has put together to
help you tweak Windows. There's an image resizer that enables
you to change the size of a photo with a single click; an
improved Calculator; a slide show generator that turns photo CDs
into on-screen slideshows; and there are utilities for colour
management, copying files from digital cameras and magnifying
sections of the screen. Best of all, though, is TweakUI. This lets
you tweak hidden settings in Windows, from the way things
appear on screen to whether Windows should delete your web
browsing history when you switch off your PC.

Acrobat Reader

www.adobe.com

If you download the Google Pack you'll get Adobe's Acrobat
Reader as part of the package, but if you don't it's worth
downloading in its own right. Reader enables you to view PDF
(Portable Document Format) files, which you'll often find on
websites: for example, the government publishes a lot of its
official forms online in PDF format, and many companies use
PDF to publish product brochures and manuals. Just last week
we had a problem with our gas boiler, checked the
manufacturer's website, downloaded the PDF manual and
discovered what the problem was – and how to fix it.

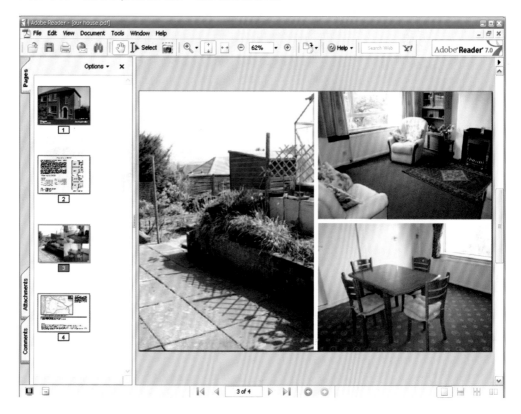

Appendix 3
User accounts

Windows is customisable in all manner of ways, from the background picture on your Desktop to the colours used on screen and the way files and folders are displayed. With user accounts, it's even possible to set up a single computer to look and behave quite differently depending upon who's using it at the time. Stuffy dad may want a business-orientated machine with a minimum of frills and distractions; teenage son may prefer a Britney background and a focus on high-speed internet gaming; studious daughter may wish to ensure that her research files are not accidentally deleted by her careless brother (and perhaps keep him away from her private diary). User accounts let each member of the family arrange things entirely to their own suiting without affecting how others use the computer. What's more, each user account is protected with a password so the kids can't muck up dad's settings (and, to some extent, vice versa).

One for all the family

There are two levels of user accounts: *Administrator*, where the user can make system-wide changes, including installing and uninstalling programs; and *Limited*, where the user can make changes to his or her own account but not interfere with the computer's main settings. We'll assume in the following example that you are the administrator. Let's now set up a limited account for Jack, your son.

① Start

Control Panel

User Accounts icon

Owner icon

First, you need to set up your own account. Click Owner to open a window where you can make changes to the account. As the sole user of the computer, you automatically have an Administrator account.

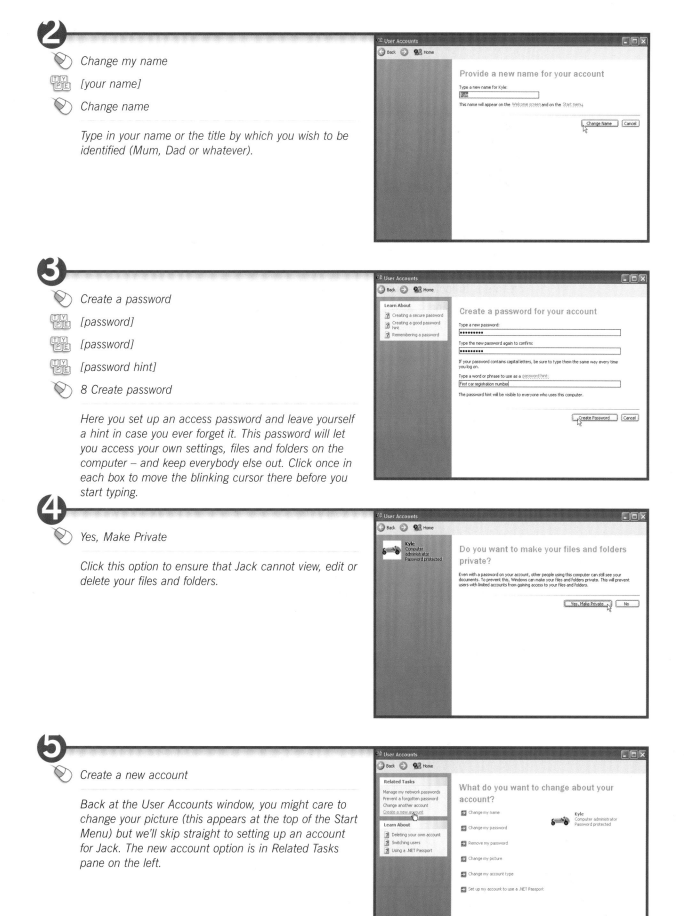

2

🖱 *Change my name*

⌨ *[your name]*

🖱 *Change name*

Type in your name or the title by which you wish to be identified (Mum, Dad or whatever).

3

🖱 *Create a password*

⌨ *[password]*

⌨ *[password]*

⌨ *[password hint]*

🖱 *8 Create password*

Here you set up an access password and leave yourself a hint in case you ever forget it. This password will let you access your own settings, files and folders on the computer – and keep everybody else out. Click once in each box to move the blinking cursor there before you start typing.

4

🖱 *Yes, Make Private*

Click this option to ensure that Jack cannot view, edit or delete your files and folders.

5

🖱 *Create a new account*

Back at the User Accounts window, you might care to change your picture (this appears at the top of the Start Menu) but we'll skip straight to setting up an account for Jack. The new account option is in Related Tasks pane on the left.

6

Jack

Next

Limited

Create Account

In the next window, type in the account name: Jack, in this example. In the following window, check the Limited account option and then click Create Account.

7

Jack icon

You are now back at main User Account window. Click the icon for Jack's account and, as in Step 3 above, give Jack his own password – or, if you trust him, leave the room and let him set his own password and password hint.

8

Choose the way users log on or off

Apply Options

Back at the main window again, click the logging on configuration option and ensure that both options are checked (they should be by default). Now close the User Accounts window and leave Control Panel.

9

Start

Log Off

Switch User

Let's see it in action. Click Log Off in the Start Menu followed by Switch User. Now Jack can log in to his account and set up Windows to his own liking without affecting your settings. You don't even have to close any programs you have running when switching accounts – they will still be running when you return. This is obviously a whole lot easier than turning your computer off and back on again.

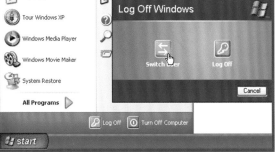

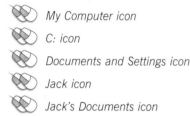 Jack icon

[Type] [password] [Enter]

Jack simply clicks his icon, types in his password and presses the Enter key to access his account. To return to your account, repeat Step 9 from within Jack's account and click your own icon. Also, whenever you or Jack turns the computer off, the first thing you'll see when you turn it back on again is a Windows welcome screen that lets you choose who should log on first.

Points to note

Because you selected the privacy option in Step 4, Jack cannot see any of your files. However, Windows has a Shared Documents folder for the express purpose of letting you share certain files. Any file in here can be accessed by all account holders regardless of whether they have Administrator or Limited account status. You'll find the Shared Documents in the Other Places part of the My Documents window.

Furthermore, because you have an Administrator account, you can see all Jack's files (although it's not immediately obvious how). Follow this procedure:

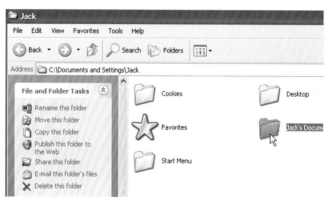

My Computer icon

C: icon

Documents and Settings icon

Jack icon

Jack's Documents icon

It takes a lot of double-clicking but eventually you arrive at Jack's own My Documents folder. This is quite distinct from yours.

Now that Jack and you have separate accounts, you each can arrange your Desktop, files, folders and personal settings however you like. Chances are that Jack's computer (so to speak) will end up looking remarkably different from your own. We're not going to look at how to customise Windows any further in this manual – it's hardly an essential part of home computing – but take it from us that Jack will know just what to do.

Appendix 4
Trouble-shooting

We have already covered different ways to keep Windows running smoothly, notably by installing updates and making well-timed restore points. However, should all go pear-shaped, there is plenty more you can do. Here we consider a couple of options.

Help and Support Center

Windows can attempt to find and resolve hardware or software problems automatically, which is ideal if the internal machinations of your system are something of a mystery.

1

Start

Help and Support

Use Tools to view your computer information and

diagnose problems.

Pretty obvious so far.

2

My Computer Information

View the status of my system hardware and software

When you make this choice, Windows analyses the current condition of your computer.

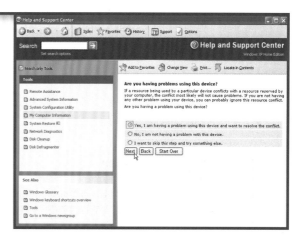

[appropriate option]

After a minute or two, you'll see a report like this, broken down into sections. At this point, you can click the Trouble-shooter option next to whichever area is causing concern. If, for instance, your computer refuses to play any sounds, click the Sound Card Trouble-shooter; or if the monitor starts displaying weird colours, click the Video Card option.

[appropriate responses]

What follows is a question-and-answer session. It can get a little confusing but take your time and read the messages carefully. Results are not guaranteed, unfortunately, but Windows will have a pretty good bash at resolving the problem.

Alternatively, you can type keywords into the Help and Support Center's internal search engine. This should take you directly to relevant information.

Note the link at the bottom of the left pane to something called the Microsoft Knowledge Base. This is a truly massive repository of helpful information on the web that goes well beyond the scope of the Help topics built into Windows itself. To access the Knowledge Base, search for help on your keywords as above *while your computer is online*, and then click the link. Now you can select articles in the left pane and read them in full in the right pane. Bear in mind that this does rather presuppose that you have a working internet connection!

The Knowledge Base has been compiled over many years and it covers all versions of Windows, so include the term 'XP' in your keywords to increase relevancy. It also tends to get very technical at times, so take a deep breath before wading in.

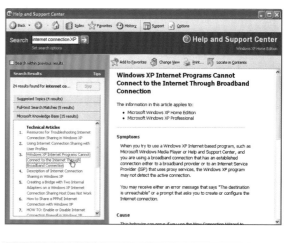

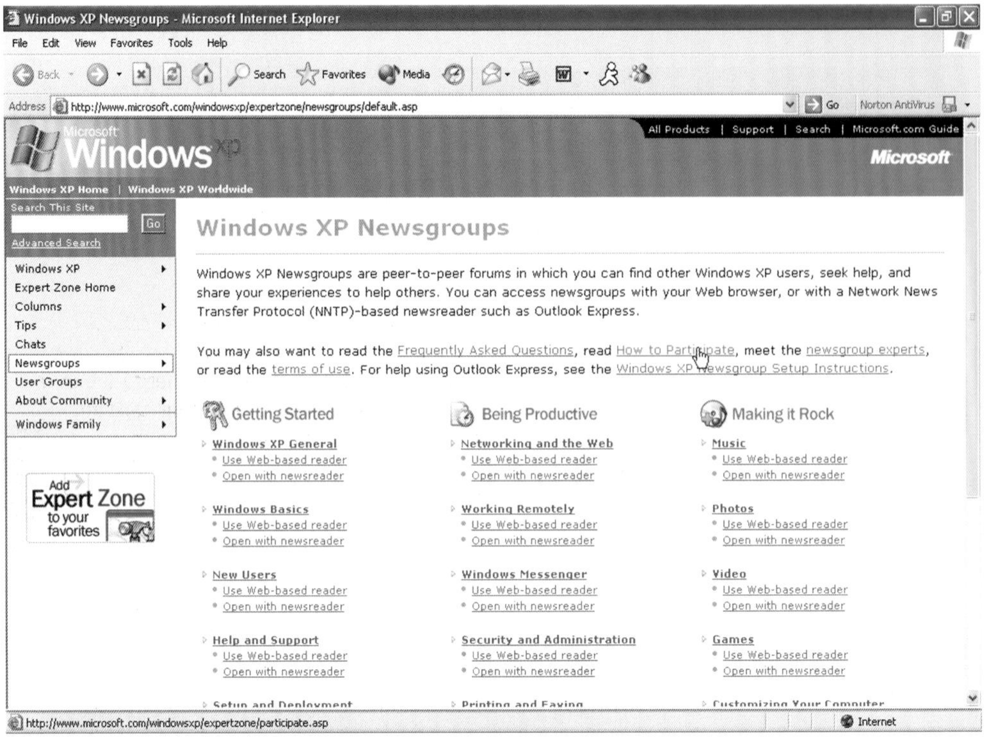

Newsgroups

Still no luck? Well, again assuming that you can get your computer online, you could try asking fellow computer owners for help. Newsgroups are discussion groups in which people exchange messages (often in rather robust language and with a fair degree of attitude, it has to be said), and there are plenty devoted to Windows, hardware and software issues. You can browse existing discussions to see if your particular problem is discussed, or you can post your own request for assistance and wait for a response (it may not be immediate, but you will get one).

You can access the Windows XP-specific newsgroups in two ways. The short route is by launching Internet Explorer and going straight to the following web page:

www.microsoft.com/windowsxp/expertzone/newsgroups/default.asp

Alternatively, do this:

Start

Help and Support

Get support, or find information in Windows XP newsgroups

Go to a Windows Web site forum

Go to Windows Newsgroups

This will launch Internet Explorer and find the relevant page.

Once there, take the time to read the 'Frequently Asked Questions' section and the bit on 'How to Participate'.

Above all, remember to back up your important files regularly. Even in the worst eventuality, you need never lose your work.

Glossary

Here we explain some of the terms mentioned but not really explored in the main part of the manual.

4.1/5.1 When an audio signal is split into several discrete channels and played back over correctly positioned speakers, the listener feels literally surrounded by sound (hence the term surround sound). A 4.1 speaker system uses four satellite speakers (two stereo speakers to the front and two behind) plus a subwoofer. In a 5.1 system, there is an additional central channel/speaker devoted to spoken dialogue in movie soundtracks.

A 4.1 speaker set up for surround sound.

Always-on In the context of broadband, a fixed internet connection that does not rely upon a modem dialling an ISP over a telephone line. You can leave an always-on connection active around the clock without racking up telephone charges.

Analogue A signal that varies continuously over time. For example, when a person speaks, the sound wave is an analogue signal, varying smoothly as they talk. Think of the hands on a traditional clock.

Background A program that works in the background is not obvious to the user (i.e. it doesn't appear in a window).

Bad old days Before Windows came DOS, a text-based operating system for personal computers. DOS is a mystery to most of us. Praise be for that.

Binary data A computer stores information in a coded form that involves nothing but long strings of 1s and 0s (i.e. it uses the binary numbering system).

Bit The smallest chunk of computer code, or data, consisting of a single 1 or 0.

Examples of buttons

Broken In the context of the web, a broken page has a problem which prevents it from being displayed properly in the browser. This could be a fault with the way the page has been coded or a blip with the server on which it is held.

Button An element of a program designed to look like a button. You can point at and click buttons with the mouse, at which point something will happen.

Cable Broadband internet access is often available through the same fibre-optic cables used to bring television and telephone services to homes and businesses.

A recordable CD drive gives you better backup options – and makes audio CDs to boot.

CD burning The process of saving files to a compact disc. Commercial CDs are pressed, much like vinyl records of old, but a computer drive uses a laser to burn a pattern onto the surface of the disc.

CD-R CD-Recordable. Recordable CDs can be filled with files once and once only.

CD-ROM CD-Read-Only Memory. Files can be read *from* a CD-ROM disc but you cannot record, or save, files to the disc.

CD-RW CD-ReWriteable. Rewriteable CDs can be filled with files repeatedly. Old files can be deleted to make space for new ones.

Check To check an option is to turn a particular feature on. To uncheck it is to turn that feature off.

Copy To copy a file is to create an exact digital duplicate of it without in any way affecting the original file.

CRT Cathode Ray Tube. A glass tube used to produce an image on some television sets and some computer monitors.

A CRT monitor.

Data Any bit or collection of information used by or stored on a computer.

Default In the context of computing, a default option is selected automatically. For instance, a printer might print in draft mode by default. The use of 'default' implies that an alternative is available.

Delete To delete a file is to remove all record of it from a hard disk or other storage media. In practice, deleted files are not physically removed until some fresh file is allocated to the same disk space. This is why deleted files can often be 'magically' recovered.

Diagnostic utility A program that attempts to find and resolve problems with your computer.

Dialogue box A window used by Windows to proffer information, offer choices and invite responses.

Dial-up An internet connection that relies upon a modem making a successful data call to an ISP over a telephone line.

An external modem.

Digital In contrast to analogue, a digital signal is composed of discrete packets of information (i.e. it moves sharply between fixed values. In terms of data, the digital data that your computer works with is 'simply' a string of 1s and 0s).

Disc/disk Disc is used with reference to *optical* storage media, such as a compact disc, and disk with reference to *magnetic* media, as in a floppy or hard disk.

Domain The top-level name of a website.

Download To download something is to transfer a copy of it from one computer to your own, especially but not exclusively across the internet.

Drive activity light A warning light that illuminates when a drive is busy working with data. The system unit has such a light, as do most CD/DVD drives. You should never remove a floppy disk while the light is on.

DSL Digital Subscriber Line. A technology that converts an ordinary household telephone line into a broadband internet connection. ADSL is most common version in the UK (the A stands for Asymmetric), with which you can download data faster than you can upload it (hence the asymmetry).

DVD movie A movie distributed on a DVD disc, as opposed to, for instance, a video cassette. A DVD drive with the right software, video card and sound card can play DVD movies on a computer.

DVD-ROM Just like CD-ROM, this is a 'read only' medium. DVD discs look just like compact discs but can hold much more data.

DVI Digital Visual Interface. A standard used to connect digital monitors to computers. A digital monitor can broadcast the pure digital signal generated by the computer's video card, with a resultant improvement in quality over that of analogue monitors, where the signal must first be converted from digital to analogue.

Don't forget to install a software player if you want to watch movies on your computer.

Ethernet A high-speed standard used to connect computers with cables in a network.

File-sharing In the context of the internet, file-sharing involves making selected files on your computer available to other people, usually anonymously. File-sharing gained notoriety when it proved an immensely popular way of swapping pirated material, particularly music.

Gigabyte A measure of data size. One Gigabyte is 1,024 Megabytes.

Hacker Somebody with the ability or aspiration to break into your computer through the internet, illegally.

Help menu In the context of a program, this is a (usually) searchable index of common questions and answers. If you get stuck, look for a Help button on the program Toolbar.

Hit In the context of search engines, a hit is a web page that contains some or all of your keywords.

There's no getting away from it: LCD monitors are infinitely sleeker and sexier than their CRT cousins.

Hyperlink An element on a web page that, if clicked, opens another web page in your browser.

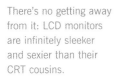

Icon A small image used by Windows to identify a file or program.

Instant chat/

instant messenger An instant messenger program lets you conduct real-time two-way text conversations (called chat) across the internet. Windows comes with its own instant messenger – look in All Programs for Windows Messenger.

Interface In the context of software, the 'look and feel' of a program, such as its buttons, menus and windows. In hardware terms, it usually refers to a physical connection, like the USB interface.

Kilobyte A measure of data size. One Kilobyte is 1024 bytes (and one byte is 8 bits).

LCD Liquid Crystal Display. A technology used to create flat-screen monitors that are much slimmer and lighter than CRT monitors.

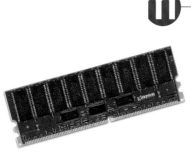

A RAM module.

Megabyte A measure of data size. One Megabyte is 1,024 Kilobytes.

Memory Memory is used to describe physical storage areas in a computer (i.e. places where data is saved). This includes Random Access Memory (RAM), which a computer uses as a temporary storage area. While you work on a letter with a word processor program, for example, the letter is 'held in RAM', and will be lost if the computer is turned off. If you save that letter, however, the file is allocated a chunk of hard disk space – another type of memory – and can be retrieved at any time.

Menu In the context of computers, a list of options from which you make a selection.

MIDI Musical Instrument Digital Interface. A standard for controlling and playing electronic musical instruments with a computer.

Modem A device that allows two computers to communicate with each other over a telephone line.

Motherboard The main circuit board inside a computer. Every other component connects to and communicates through the motherboard.

Multimedia A combination of text, sound, pictures and video.

Network Any two or more computers connected together equals a network. They can be connected with cables, wirelessly, directly, or remotely. The internet is, of course, the grand-daddy of networks.

Newsgroups Discussion groups on the internet where you can post messages, read replies from other people, and exchange files. Outlook Express can be set up to access newsgroups but you should first check whether your ISP provides access to this part of the internet (which is known as Usenet).

Online gaming You can play computer games against strangers over the internet. A broadband connection helps enormously.

Online shopping You can buy stuff from virtual shops, like Amazon.com, over the internet. You can even have your groceries delivered to your door.

Overtype To overtype is to replace old text with new text without deleting the old text first. You can generally do this when the old text is highlighted.

Parallel port A single socket on the back of a computer typically used to connect a printer (before USB took over).

Parental controls Any software measure that lets somebody control, limit, supervise or otherwise modify the way somebody else uses a computer, particularly with regard to the internet.

Plug-and-play A standard that enables a computer running Windows to automatically recognise and configure a new hardware device.

Plug it in and play straight away.

Pop-up A menu that just 'pops up' on screen.

Processor A silicon chip that processes data very, very quickly. Effectively, the brain of your computer.

Product Activation Certain Microsoft programs, including Windows XP, must be activated to keep them working beyond a certain cut-off period. This anti-piracy measure essentially involves sending a code to Microsoft (anonymously) that ties the software to your particular computer and prevents you or anybody else from installing it on multiple computers. It's controversial, but the process itself is very straightforward, particularly if you have an internet connection.

Restart To restart a computer is to turn it off and on again immediately.

Satellite Broadband internet access is available through a similar kind of satellite service that brings television to the home. It's worth considering if you can't otherwise get DSL or cable broadband, but still very expensive.

Secure In terms of the internet, a secure website is one where confidential information, such as your credit card number, is encrypted at the point of sending. Basically, it means it's safe to shop.

Select To select something is, generally speaking, to click it. Once selected, an object becomes active (i.e. the focus of current activity).

Serial A pair (usually) of ports on the back of a computer once used to connect devices like mice and modems, but now increasingly obsolete.

Serial ports

Server A computer that is linked, directly or indirectly, to other computers and can be accessed by them. Servers are commonly used for large-scale data storage. The web consists of thousands of servers on which web pages are stored.

Session In computer-speak, a session is a period spent doing something or other. An internet session is a period spent online, for example.

Sound card An expansion card that lets a computer make sounds (providing there are speakers attached), particularly useful for playing music and games.

Streaming Streaming sound and video files are downloaded to your computer piece by piece. This means that you can start listening or watching them without having to wait for the whole file to download first.

A sound card.

Subwoofer A speaker designed to broadcast very low-frequencies. An integral part of a surround sound system.

Surfing To surf is to visit web pages and click on links.

Surround sound See 4.1/5.1.

A scanner.

t

Technical support Virtually all ISPs offer some form of technical support by telephone by which you can call them up to seek assistance. This is often charged at premium rates, however. In many cases, you'll find that the ISP's customers are only too happy to pool resources and offer advice for free, often in newsgroups (see the entry above).

TWAIN A standard that get scanners talking to and working with programs. It's not an acronym, unfortunately, although urban legend insists it was coined for Technology Without An Interesting Name (we're happy to keep the myth alive).

u

USB connectors.

USB Universal Serial Bus. A fast interface with which peripherals can connect to a computer. The beauty of USB is that it's hot-swappable, which means you can unplug one device and plug in another without restarting Windows. Now in its second, much faster incarnation, called USB 2.0.

User licence The terms and conditions governing ownership and use of a software program. Read a user licence once, just for kicks.

v

VGA Video Graphics Array. The most basic standard governing a video card's output and a monitor's display capability. Also used to describe the hardware connection between the card and monitor.

Video card An expansion card that lets a computer generate images on a monitor.

w

Web forums Discussion groups contained within websites. All you need to take part is a browser.

Web page A document stored on an internet server that can be viewed by anyone with an internet connection and a browser.

Web space A chunk of reserved hard disk space on an internet server whereon you can design a web page or site. Most ISPs give you a few Megabytes of web space for free, which is ample to build a sizeable website.

Web-based e-mail An e-mail service where you send and collect messages through your browser. Because web-based e-mail is independent of ISPs (i.e. it doesn't matter how you happen to be connected to the internet at the time) it is ideal for sending and picking up messages from anywhere in the world, particularly when travelling.

z

Zipping Compressing a file to reduce the space it takes up.

Index

ACKNOWLEDGEMENTS

Author	**Kyle MacRae**
Project Manager	**Louise McIntyre**
Design	**Simon Larkin**
Copy editor	**John Hardaker**
Page build	**James Robertson**
Photography	**Tom Bain**
Illustrations	**Matthew Marke**
Index	**Nigel d'Auvergne**